The Eyes (

The Eyes of Light

by

Henri Le Saux

(Swami Abhishiktananda)

DIMENSION BOOKS
DENVILLE, NEW JERSEY

The texts of this volume, first published in English by Dimension Books, Inc., P.O. Box 811, Denville, New Jersey 07834 were selected and presented by André Gozier and Joseph Lemarié who offer the following editorial note:

We wish to express our thanks to Madame O. Baumer for the unpublished texts that she has so kindly made available to us as well as to the Abhishiktananda Society for its generous cooperation with our endeavor. We likewise thank the editors of reviews who have authorized us to publish articles by Father Le Saux which have previously appeared in their pages but are little known. Finally, we thank the addressees of the letters published in the book for permitting us to present them to the public.

Father Le Saux's lines of research are by now known. Unfortunately, it had not been possible for him to complete the editing of these texts, most often unpublished, for the results of his research were not directly intended for publication. Such, at least, was the case with most of them. Despite their fragmentary character, they highly merit inclusion in the record of the dialogue between Christians and Indians. These essays are presented here in this perspective of research. This explains some expressions, some pages that might baffle or bother some readers, but it is not possible to transform the texts of a deceased author. One can only recommend to such readers his other books so that the nuances of his thought can be fully and properly grasped.

Table of Contents

ARTICLES IN PERIODICALS

Supplement of *La Vie spirituelle, Monachisme Chrétien aux Indes,* t. 9 (Christian monasticism in India), September 1956.

L'hindouisme est-il toujours vivant? (Is Hinduism still alive?) in *Vitalité actuelle des religions non chrétiennes, Rencontres* 48, Paris, 1957, and in *Vie intellectuelle,* November 1956.

La Vie spirituelle, Swami Pamara Arubi Anandam, Jules Monchanin, January 1958.

CARMEL, Tarascon, Bouches-du-Rhone.

1965/I: *L'Inde et le Carmel* (India and the Carmelite Order), p. 9.

1965/II: *L'Inde et le Carmel,* continuation and conclusion, p. 109.

1966/IV: *Le prêtre que l'Inde attend, que le monde attend* (The priest for whom India waits, for whom the world waits), p. 270.

Vie thérésienne, 33, rue du Carmel, 14100 Lisieux. *"Femmes ermites hindoues* (Hindu women hermits), January 1970.

Annales de sainte Thérèse de Lisieux, 33, rue du Carmel, 14100 Lisieux.

January 1970: *Gandhi, Témoin de la Verite* (Ghandi, Witness of Truth).
January 1972: *Enfance spirituelle et Upanishads* (Spiritual infancy and Upanishads).

April 1972: *Pélerinages himalayens* (Himalayan pilgrimages).

BOOKS BY FATHER HENRI LE SAUX

Ermites du Saccidananda, in collaboration with Father Monchanin, an attempt at a Christian integration of India's monastic tradition, Casterman, 1956.

*Sagesse hindous, mystique chrétienne, Du Vedanta a la Trinit*é (Hindu wisdom, Christian mysticism, from the Vedanta to the Trinity), Centurion, 1956.

Recontre de l'hindouisme et du christianisme (Encounter between Hinduism and Christianity), Seuil, 1966.

Une messe aux sources du Gange (A Mass at the sources of the Ganges), Seuil, 1967.

Gnânânanda, *un maître spirituel du Pays tamoul* (a spiritual teacher of the Tamil Country), an evocative account of the spiritual milieu of southern India, Chambéry, Éditions Présence, 1970.

Éveil à soi, éveil à Dieu, (Awakening to self, awakening to God). Taken from an essay in English: *Prayer,* 1967, Centurion, 1971.

Souvenirs d'Arunâchala (Memories of Arunachala), account of a Christian hermit on Hindu soil, Editions de l'Épi, 1978.

There remain numerous unpublished texts responsibility for the publication of which has been assumed by the Abhishiktananda Society, Rev. J.D.M. Stuart, Brotherhood House, 7 Court Lane, Delhi 110054, and by O. Baumer, particularly the journal.

Brief Biography

of

Father Henri Le Saux, OSB
Swami Abhishiktananda

Born on August 30, 1910 in Saint-Briac, near Saint-Malo (Ille-et-Vilaine).

Attended the *Grand Seminaire* of Rennes.

Made his profession in the Benedictine Order at the Benedictine Abbey of Kergonan (Morbihan) on May 17, 1931.

Ordained as priest on December 21, 1935.

Functioned as Master of Ceremonies, Professor of Church History, Canon Law and Patristics.

Very early, he heard an inner call to India. He got in touch with *Abbé* Jules Monchanin in 1947 and joined him in India in 1947. Sharing the same contemplative ideal, very conscious of the spiritual riches of India, they founded a hermitage in the diocese of Tiruchirapalli: the ashram of Saccidananda in Kulittali (province of Madurai). Father Le Saux more often called it Shantivanam (abbreviated SH or SHV): "Wood of Peace." The hermitage (a chapel, three cells) is situated in the middle of a grove of mango trees on the banks of the Kavery. *Abbé* Monchanin died on October 10, 1957. After making a pilgrimage to the sources of the Ganges in the spring of 1959, Dom Le Saux dreamed of returning there. He set up a small hermitage in Uttarkashi, not far from the sources of the Ganges, in 1962. It is there that he wrote his chief works. Previously, he had participated in the Ecumenical Assembly of 1961, and in several seminars devoted to theological reflection in northern and southern India. Before these seminars, he had shared the life of the *Sannyasis* in the famous holy mountain of Arunachala (Tamil Nad) and thus also came to know firsthand the life of the itinerant Sadhou, Father Francis Mahieu and Bede Griffith, having taken over his duties at the ashram.

Suffered a heart attack in Rishikesh in July 1975.

Died in the Catholic Hospital of Indorf on December 7, 1973.

Buried in the cemetery of the Fathers of the Divine Word in Dolda, near Indore.

The Eyes of Light

FOREWORD

The published works of Father Le Saux/Swami Abhishiktananda have already drawn the attention of the general public to this monastic personage who, in the words uttered by Father Monchanin on his death bed, has fathomed the mystery of India more deeply than anyone else before him. He left behind numerous unpublished manuscripts and, thanks to his family and to Mme. O. Baumer, we are happy to be able to publish some of them. This book includes a summary of his biographical data (those interested in further details can consult the article in the *Dictionnaire de Spiritualité,* D.S. Col. 697-698, vol. IX, written by Father Lemarié) and lists a bibliography of the works that have appeared in French. It should be stressed that Dom Le Saux's writings sprang directly from his experience. In the wake of the call that summoned Monchanin to India, Lebbe to China, Peyriguère to Morocco, Beaurecueil to Afghanistan—not to mention others of whom there were so many—Father Henri Le Saux also heard a call, but this time one that was monastic, purely monastic, summoning him to India: "Come" He followed this voice and stayed in India until his death.

In this Foreword we feel that we could do no better than to reproduce the letter Father Le Saux addressed to Father Monchanin on August 18, 1947. "You climb, you descend, you no longer see, but you have seen." This is also the moment when doubts and hesitations set in. But the desire remains and it is the desire that is the driving force insofar as it progressively inflames the heart and illumines the world and gives one courage to take chances. In the end, anyone who should one day look squarely into the face of somebody who has lived with this "beyondness"—so far as it is possible for a human being to judge it—and who has arrived at his destination, at this "point of trespass," will be able to bear witness that he has experienced a deep personal and soul-filled Presence and that in this contact he has also opened himself more deeply to The Presence of God Himself.

Letter to Father Monchanin

Sainte-Anne-de-Kergonan
(Ploucharnel, Morbihan)
August 18, 1947

Dear Father,

Your letter was a great joy to me and I too wonder whether I should not consider it as a response from on high. For I finally see that the work which for so long a time was the object of my most ardent aspirations, namely, the establishment of the monastic life in India, is in the process of being realized and that, perhaps, I myself will have the good fortune to participate in it.

This has been my dream, in fact, for more than thirteen years, and in these last years it has been with me incessantly, as thought and prayer. In the past two years I have obtained permission from my Superior to make some inquiries in this direction. I have received much encouragement, but once it becomes a question of actualizing the plan difficulties arise and the proferred aid vanishes. First of all, I contacted the Abbé Dom Néve, and everything progressed smoothly and quite far. But from the moment that I made it clear that my aim was an essentially contemplative life, and not a semi-contemplative, semi-apostolic life, Dom Néve replied that it would be better if each one separately experimented on his own (at that time he already had some proposals in connection with Colombo). At the same time, I exchanged several letters with Bishop de Pondichéry and Bishop de Salem. The latter's response, above all, was enthusiastic. Only his diocese had been created all too recently and, besides, it was too poor to assume responsibility for such a foundation. Thus, after several months of hope, every letter I received begot only a new disappointment. Among them, however, arrived one that was a source of joy: a much beloved brother (of my monastery), unasked, offered to join me and, instinctively, I

9

knew that with him the communion of heart and mind would be total. So I again approached Bishop Kierkels, the apostolic delegate. His response was very warm-hearted but he postponed any consideration of my project until his return from Europe (toward the end of this year, I think) should he by then, and at all events, see an opportunity to turn my desire into something useful. It was still quite problematical, and I put out a last feeler—I had pretty much decided to give up the whole project if this too proved to be fruitless, for I could not live indefinitely in this state of uncertainty. I was quite aware of the Christian vitality of Madurai. I had read Bishop Mendocia's interview, to which I referred the other day, in *La Croix* last November. So, on the feast of the Ascension, I wrote this last letter and mailed it on the following day after first having deposited it on the altar during the vigil I keep every evening in front of the Tabernacle, repeating our *Suscipe* with a view to India—I had been waiting for an answer since mid-June. I began to think that the Lord did not want me for India and once again I gave up my study of English, of the Tamil language and of the Upanishads, since I was unable to sacrifice immediately useful occupations to these studies that increasingly risked being of no further use. And your letter arrived on the day after the Feast of Our Lady!

It really would have been wonderful had we been able to meet in the course of your trip to France. But why grieve over what the Lord has permitted? It would, in fact, have been so simple for Him to bring us together. For more than a year had passed since I had asked my Superior for permission to track down your whereabouts. However, I did not know that you were thinking of the establishment of Hindu monasticism. All I knew was that, as a French priest, you were in India trying, in the light of Christ, to fathom the truths, profound and so beautiful, hidden in Hindu speculation. I had learned about this thanks to an article by Father

Danielou in *Études* (a fleeting reference). Later, in an advertisement I came upon the title of your article in *Dieu vivant* (but being a "poor" monk it was impossible for me to acquire it). But then I had the joy of discovering this article in a pre-war issue of *Contemplation et Apostolat* (practically the same, if I judge it by the critical comment of the *Revue Thomiste*. I say "joy" because it did me much good to meet someone who loved India and who had penetrated to the deepest levels of her thought with so much Christian sympathy—something which for several years had been my dearest occupation. Just imagine! To find someone whom the thought of the Atman* leads to the contemplation of the Divine Advocate and who feels, beyond the surface pantheism, the intuition of it possessed by the great seers of the Upanishads. It is tantamount to telling you how, without knowing each other, we were already in a great communion of heart and mind as regards our beloved India. To be sure, I had neither the time nor the means to push my Indianist formation beyond an altogether elementary initiation, but what I have achieved, assuredly, is firmly anchored in me: a deep love for India, an intense intellectual sympathy for her thought. In other words, I am telling you how happy I would be if my joining you should turn out to be feasible.

You speak of probable disappointments. I expect as much and the Lord, in order to prepare me for them, has not spared me from experiencing them during these last years. I have looked squarely in the face at a good number of them as well as at a good number of obstacles. I am aware of my weakness, of course, but I have confidence in the strength of the Holy Spirit. Nevertheless I would like you to reassure me, before all else, on one point, on the likely usefulness of the

---

*The essence in man identical with the essence of the universe. (Tr.)

envisioned work. Is there really a well-grounded hope that
souls can be found capable of responding to the monastic
ideal that we expect to propose to them! On this score,
Bishop Prunier has unhesitatingly given me assurances. I
have read the same in many reviews, for example. You live
there, you are immediately affected by the question: what do
you think of it? Here India, her land and her peoples, her
heart and mind, appears to us enveloped in a halo of poetry.
Thus, in principle, we might tend to be very careful in this
matter with regard to illusion. And there is another consideration: the ongoing experiments in the same direction.
Bishop Kierkels wrote me that at the present time there are
two experiments, a work being undertaken by religious who
have been in India for a long time and which has already been
proposed to Rome . . . [a whole sentence is missing here
because of the wear and tear of the paper] . . . I've heard (in
regard to India) about some Benedictines who might be
establishing themselves in the Travancore (Visancya Ypuram)
(but I think theirs would be a European-style house). There is
above all the community of Rosarians of Jaffna the recruit-
ment for which is carried out primarily, I believe, in Madurai.
In that case, is there room for another viable project? For,
even though I deeply love "sacred India," even though her
call fills me with anguish, even though there is nothing about
the eremetic life over there (in the event of failure) that
displeases me, I am duty-bound to be mindful of my present
situation, as a member of a monastery.

Now I believe it is proper to lay before you the fun-
damentals of the plans to which my readings and reflections
have led me. To be sure, I do not wish to establish anything *a
priori*, for the supreme law that guides me is adaptation to
circumstances, submission to the real. I already mentioned
them sketchily in a few lines in my letter of May 15.[1] Here
they are in a slightly more developed form. You will let me
know what you think of them and whether they fit in with
your views.

First of all, and here we are certainly in complete agreement, total Indianization: I am absolutely sure of sharing your thoughts on this matter, however radical they may be. Nevertheless, in my opinion, the point of departure should be the Rule of St. Benedict because it had behind it an extremely reliable monastic tradition which would prevent a headlong plunge into the unknown. But it must be the Rule as such, separated from the developments that the modern age has, at times, constrained it to undergo, with its original character, so flexible and universal. I should like to propose to our dear Tamils the Rule in its nascent state, so to speak, so that customs proper to Hinduism can gradually be grafted onto it by way of experience, the only teacher. But, on this foundation, like yourself, I see a re-flowering of the so variegated monastic tree, the hermits, the anchorites, the mendicants. There is all of India's contemplative thrust to be sanctified, and there are the monastic institutions in which India expresses her profound soul, to be Christianized. And I see developing around the monastery, the indispensable center of these various monastic activities, to which the brothers called to a more special vocation would come to acquire new strength, a very Hindu adaptation of the Benedictine oblation and of Benedictine hospitality in the form of an ashram where pagans and Christians alike would come in search of nourishment for their spiritual life. I believe that the Benedictine Rule, in its marvelous profundity and stability, is pliant enough to dominate all these monastic forms, as it has done elsewhere in its heyday. I became very sure of this quite recently while preparing a lecture on ancient and medieval monastic history. You will easily understand, moreover, that eighteen years of Benedictine life have deeply bound me to the *sancta regula*, that my dream is to give new children to our Founder who will fashion Christian India just as their elder brothers fashioned Christian Europe. The prospect that one day you and I together, as I ardently hope, will voice and exchange interesting views on this matter, about which we shall surely agree, is once more proved to me by your article.

I should like to preserve in a very particular way the non-clerical character of the original Rule. Clericalism has restricted the appeal of monastic life, or rather the response of the monastic institute to the contemplative possibilities of the Christian soul. The conventual prayer naturally will be recited in the Tamil language because it must be the well-spring and the exquisite fruit of the private prayer that fills the day. At the traditional hours, manual work shall be suspended (here again it is just a matter of applying the Holy Rule) not as a mechanical copying of the monastic regimen but as a wise adaptation of it, with readings based on the psalter, the scriptural Canticles, other parts of the Bible, the Fathers, or the Lives of Saints. And in the place of our magnificent but untranslatable hymns, why not admit the suitable Hindu mystic compositions? If St. Gregory ordered Augustine of Canterbury to preserve the temples of the idols for Christ, could we not also preserve for Christ the beautiful accents that inspire Hindu poets with their deep love of God, even if it is externalized in the appeals to Shiva or to Kali?

You certainly must know about the Chinese experience of Father Lebbe, whom I love to call the most authentic disciple of St. Benedict in our times! His success, on the very bases that I am proposing, is very characteristic. On the other hand, compared to him, foundations in which there had been an excessive desire to copy mechanically what is European or the Benedictinism of the 20th century, vegetate.

The observance will certainly be very austere, much more so than in our French monasteries. I have no objection to that. On the contrary! As you tell me and as formerly did Nobilli, Brito and their followers, one must live as a *sannyasi*[2] and this way of life is a Hindu institution with its traditional rules to which one must submit. This does not mean to say that it will be necessary to compete with the pagan ascetics.

On the contrary, it will be necessary—as Benedict did former-ly—to show the primordial value of the interior life and the accidental role of the worldly life. Nevertheless, there is a minimum that we will be required to observe. And here experience alone will still be the teacher. And the Lord will give us the necessary strength.

Thank God, I enjoy excellent health, although the regularity of monastic life has not habituated my health to harsh blows of any kind. I am at a favorable age (37) . . . but I put trust in the Lord, above all. Moreover, it will be possible, I think, to find a healthy and sufficiently temperate place as can be found in the first ranges of the Gathe mountains—one which does not add new difficulties or, to be more exact, which does not impose harmful exertions on the body.

Monastic life does not proceed without serious work: *otiositas inimica animae,* says St. Benedict, and history tells us that idleness is a risk incurred by Christian, pagan, occidental or oriental monasticism. In my opinion, the work must be at once intellectual and manual, according to the individual aptitudes of the monks. For my part, I much prefer intellectual work, but I think that it will be necessary to think of those brothers equipped with more modest intelligence, who nevertheless are capable of living the contemplative life. Moreover, the necessities of sheer subsistence will no doubt force us in this direction. Gandhi awaits a lesson of manual labor from Christian monks. From us the bishops await work of an entirely intellectual kind (books, reviews, newspapers without delay) and in a more general fashion, a reconsideration of the Christian dogma in the Hindu fashion, and a reconsideration of Hindu speculation in the Christian manner. And this latter work strongly tempts me. Nevertheless, whatever the work may be, I believe, in accordance with the healthiest monastic tradition, that it will have to be kept within bounds and not become an end in itself. We do not want to set up an agricultural undertaking, or a settlement, nor a dispensary for the propagation of texts, nor a university. If the Lord brings this about—and no doubt He will do so after two or three monastic generations have passed, as He did in Europe—this will be fine, indeed very fine, but that will not be our aim. We are monks only so that from here below we may enter the Kingdom of God. There is a sentence in St. Gregory's Life of St. Benedict which for me is the fundamental monastic motto: "He dwelt alone, and by himself, under the eyes of Him who looks down from above."

In order for it to be properly in order, all this social usefulness of monasticism (economic or religious or intellectual) must be a *fruit* and not an end; and the exclusively contemplative end will have to be safeguarded all the more tenaciously the more the bishops will have need of us, the more our assistance appears sovereignly useful. We shall have to defend ourselves just as we are doing in France at the present time.

I believe that after reading these pages, you will be able to surmise to some degree what I am like and therefore determine whether, in your opinion, we can make an attempt at a fruitful collaboration. I hope the answer is yes: to be sure at times I am scared and feel crushed, but the call of India is deep in me, inscribed as it is on my inmost self. Please reply in all frankness. If you believe that I can be useful to you, tell me so. And I hope that then the good Lord will grant me the means to join you without too much delay.

Now—in the event that your judgment is favorable—some practical questions would have to be dealt with: my Superior has immediately replied—via air mail, I presume—to Bishop Mendoc, requesting from him an attestation (that he would receive me) in order to solicit the indult of exclaustration which I need. He also touched on the financial aspects. The monastery—poor in itself—must make some repairs (war damages) amounting to several million francs, and therefore it can do absolutely nothing for me, neither for the journey nor for my living costs over there. And up to now the Father Superior has not yet permitted me to take any steps to solicit help.

First, the question of the journey. You have just made it yourself. Could you give me some practical information (a monk lives in a cloister and is ignorant of many matters) on how to go about things—on the price—on the possibility of getting help to defray costs? Given the climate of Madurai, what is the preferable time to arrive? what months should be avoided? From my readings I have gathered that the months from April to August are particularly unfavorable. In fact, at best, I won't be able to arrive before the end of the year. I have some work to wind up, especially putting the library in order (which only I can do quickly). We have had four years of exile and we must start from scratch. I count on two or three months to finish this work.

Second, the matter of expenses over there. First of all, the exchange rate of the franc to the rupee (or of the pound to the rupee), what possibilities are there for the transfer of funds, the drawing up of a modest budget to which necessarily must be added the costs of some excursions and some purchases of books for the necessary formation. Mass intention: what is the fee? Would it be preferable to find out about this in England or in Canada? (One dollar or a quarter of a pound). (In France at the present time it is only 80 francs). What would be a useful sum to have upon arriving over there as regards the expenses of setting up house and making the first expenditures (leaving out the Mass stipends)?

Lastly, what is one to bring in the way of luggage: don't be afraid to go into the lowliest details: undergarments, linen . . . is it better to make purchases over there? My intention is to limit to the maximum these impediments of European civilization and to content myself, as soon as possible, like the snob Lanza del Vasto, with the simple Hindu robe, even though this perhaps may not be possible right away. Judge and let me know.

For outer wear, while waiting to dress as a *sannyasi,* I would think of keeping the Benedictine habit, but in white cotton instead of black wool. Tell me what you think. Black would certainly be of no use to me over there. Would it not be better for me to have a garment in white cotton with a simple, black, light-quilted priest's overcoat, and leave these copious garments, so costly nowadays, here?

In all simplicity I await your views on all these questions along with other practical instructions that you can give me. This is only in connection with the period of transition. Nevertheless, together with this brother about whom I have told you, I dream of the day we shall be fully Tamil in our dress, in our life and in our customs, seated in the choir in the lotus pose—if ever, at least, one can really get the hang of it—and eating, squatted, on banana-tree leaves.

I must send you this letter—necessarily quite a lengthy one—by boat, inasmuch as the extra postage by air mail would be too costly. I hope nevertheless that it won't take too long and that without too great a delay I shall be able to come to a firm decision and thus—if you still believe that you can send for me—get ready for my departure.

Will you be so kind as to offer my respects to His Excellency Bishop Mendoca and thank him for the welcome that he is willing to reserve for me.

For quite a long time I have been mentioning my brothers of the Tamil country in my Mass intention. It is like telling you the place that you now occupy in this prayer: obtain for me from the Lord that He respond holily . . . . [Here the letter tears off].

                                        Henri Le Saux

PART ONE

CHAPTER 1

The Experience of God

In the Religions of the Far East[1]

The odds are dead set against anyone treating of the experience of God in the worlds of the Far East. For on the one hand, whether the subject under discussion is Vedanta, Buddhism or Tao, what is striking at first sight is that the equivalent to what in the West is called "experience of God" finds absolutely no need to achieve clarity or exactitude with respect to the idea of "God." Indeed, some traditions emphatically reject it, while others accept it only as a point of departure or, at best, as an aid along the way. On the other hand, the subject is too vast to permit anyone to have a real competence in the matter save that of an academic nature. Now, when it is a matter of experience, a competence that is simply academic does not take one very far. This observation is all the more important because it is a question here of the world of the East which, contrary to the Greek and Mediterranean world, has not accepted the primacy of the *eidos,* of the *logos,* of the idea. Rather, at all times, it has been directly drawn by Being, life, experience in itself. . . . This is why notional communication has always been considered as insufficient for the transmission of the inner mystery. There is no sense whatsoever in studying the Upanishads or the Dhammapada, the Path of Truth, solely in order to know what the *rishis* (seers) or the Buddha might have thought. For any study of the Hindu or Buddhist Scriptures which does not aim at a spiritual deepening is fundamentally invalidated.

In the Hindu tradition this experience in particular is discussed only in the "non-dual" intimacy of the "guru-disciple" relationship. The guru does not have the right to reveal its secret except to the properly prepared disciple who, at peace in his heart and free of all craving save the single craving for this experiential knowledge of being, has total faith in his guru. This very approach explains the repugnance felt by so many true Hindus for what is called the inter-religious dialogue, because of the very conditions in which it unfolds most often reduce it to the "academic plane," hence to a superficial plane.

The secret of the Upanishadic religious experience is not disclosed in conversation or in discussion, but by seating oneself humbly at the feet of a Teacher and by listening to him attentively, with a heart that is open and full of faith.

Whence arises the paradoxical situation in which one who is asked to treat of this experience in public finds himself. Nobody can really agree to talk about it save one who has only an intellectual knowledge of it—and in that case, besides words, what does one really transmit?

"He who comes back having gone but half the way comes back not."

He who knows observes silence. Or, like the Zen masters, he limits himself to tossing out some paradoxes that may open the mind of the listener and make him discern the level of his being where he is absolutely and exclusively himself.

APPROACHES TO THE INNER MYSTERY

When man tries to penetrate beyond phenomenon, condi-tioning, time, becoming—beyond that in and around his own self and in the universe—he feels himself irresistibly carried away by an unknown, ineffable source of self, of all that which is; indeed as far as a mystery more inwrought than anything that he is capable of feeling, thinking, knowing, from within or without, than anything that he can abstract or imagine. It is a beyondness that flows over from all sides, that envelops all as though from without and that, from within, is an irresistible call to dive into an ever deeper abyss, to the inmost center of self and of the world, to the point of departure and of arrival alike of all human experience. It is precisely here that two fundamental, contrasting attitudes in the spiritual history of humankind meet in the articulation of this experience of depth. I trust I shall be allowed this simplification because, as a matter of fact, these two attitudes are frequently in opposition. Nevertheless it is important to grasp them and to recognize them in their essential thrust.

THE PROPHETIC EXPERIENCE

There is the specifically religious approach called prophetic, also called "monotheistic": Man lays himself bare before Another, of an All-Other, so completely other that this other defies any definition of otherness that man can ever devise. The presence of this Other is shattering, it is pure "Transcendence." He is the Yahweh of the Bible, the Allah of the Koran. I depend totally on him. It is he who created me, he alone who maintains me in being. I depend on him totally. He created me, he alone maintains me in being, he alone can bridge this abyss which my sin has placed between him and me. The dependence is total and the distance between us is infinite. It is on the base of such an experience of God that the revelation received by Abraham is founded, the base of the entire Old Testament. Only divine love can bridge this distance between man and God. God enters into a cov-

enant with man, with a people whom He sets apart, and to
whom He gives a law and a cult as a specific sign and
guarantee of this covenant.

At the time of the Gospels, however—in the fullness of
time—there was no longer to be a simple external covenant, a
Law, a Torah, the word of God transmitted through inter-
mediaries. The Word of Yahweh, who created the world,
who bequeathed the Covenant, who spoke through the Prophets, itself becomes flesh, man, a member of the chosen
people. This infinite distance, this yawning chasm that stood
between man and God is now bridged. God sends to earth
His own Son, co-eternal, consubstantial with Himself,
uniting the mystery of God and the mystery of man, at one
and the same time, in His theandric nature. For it is necessary
that the abyss be bridged: as St. Thomas says at the beginning
of the First and Second Part of the *Summa Theologica:* Man
cannot be satisfied in the most essential aspirations of his
nature save through the vision, save through the waiting for
God in his own self.

The whole biblical and Christian tradition of the experience of God leans upon this intuition of the God-Other;
of a God who must needs bridge the abyss between Him and
us and who, to effect this, calls us to Him, permits us to
become His own children in His only begotten Son, who invites us to a union with him in a similar fashion and thus to
participate in the mystery of his intimate life that the Spirit
bequeathes to us in his very interiority. The distance is bridged;
however, it is a distance that is ever bridged. It is the *epec-
tase* [reaching *towards*] of which Gregory of Nyssa loved to
talk, and which endures throughout man's eternity. Moreover here below man is in time and becoming. He is susceptible to climbing, to falling. And he courts the risks of falling
at any moment. He must always cry out to God: *Kyrie
eleison*, Lord, have mercy!

THE EXPERIENCE OF NON-DUALITY

Over against this experience of God-Other, there is the experience that does not even allow for the possibility of recognizing this Other, either by name or by a distinguishing feature. So crushing was this experience that it brings about the feeling of an emptiness in being. Here one can recall the words of the Bible: "God is a consuming fire, none can behold him and live." And here it is not first and foremost a question of the life of the flesh. What has been consumed by the flame and what has disappeared, as it were, is its thought, its selfhood, its consciousness of being, the *I* that man thinks and pronounces throughout the day. It is no longer a question of merely saying: "Thou art all, my God, I am but naught." For as long as this naught, this presumed nothingness still says that he is nothing he still considers himself something by virtue of this very utterance. No, here there is place for naught else but silence. Not, however, the silence of someone who would have ceased to speak. Rather, it is pure and absolute silence for, as a matter of fact, there is no longer a person to speak. To set transcendence over against immanence would be absolutely insufficient, if not misleading. It is not a question here of a God who would be immanent, period. For again one must ask, immanent to whom? At bottom, moreover, true immanence and true transcendence are on a par with each other. Perfect transcendence lets nothing else subsist. The words, so forceful and so often repeated in Isaiah 2, *Ego sum Dominus et non est alius,*[2] must be understood in their most absolute sense such as is confirmed by the Upanishadic experience: *sat (atman, brahman) Ekam eva advitiyam.*[3] In this experience man is no longer able to project anyone or anything opposite to himself, or to place in any part of the Real another pole to which he would conform himself and call God. Having arrived, in effect, at the center of his inmost self, man is so seized by the mystery that thenceforth it is beyond his power to pronounce either a Thou or an I. The mystery has so engulfed him in the depths of his selfhood that it is as though he has vanished from his own sight.

The proximity of this mystery, which the prophetic tradition calls God, has too totally consumed him in its flame for him to subsist. It is not discernment of the mystery of God, the Absolute, as inwardness or as immanent to self. The abyss has disappeared in this very engulfment. The transcendence felt at this depth has emptied the beholder of his own self. The cry that would be uttered—were a cry still possible—or the cry uttered at the very moment of engulfment is . . . but there is no chasm, there is no abyss, there is no face to face, there is only This—The One who *IS* and none other to name him—*advaita*. Who even pronounced that? The one who pronounced it cannot identify himself with anyone or anything. It is pure *ASTI* (is), pure *AHAM ASMI* (I am), according to the flashing intuition of the Brihad-aranyaka Upanishad. Even *AHAM* (I) is altogether too much, for in human language *AHAM* postulates a *TVAM* (Thou). But the Westerner, unfailingly, will ask, "But is not this pure AHAM God?" Where is God? Who is God—when there is no longer anyone to name Him? It is the pure *silence* of the unnameable, unpersonifiable God discerned in the loss of one's own self at the profoundest depth of one's being.

The Great have always declined to discuss this mystery. The Buddha rejects any questions pertaining to it. Buddhist and Vedantic commentators, of course, have discoursed on that in an indefinite way; so difficult is it for the mind to remain silent. Nevertheless the fundamental intuition is silence, for once he attempts to pin down the reality that this experience has revealed, man relapses into the sphere of phenomena, of thoughts, of ideas, of signs. And no sign can penetrate into it.

The true gurus attempt first of all to actualize the great

silence in the mind of their disciples: they make them finger it: on the one hand, the impermanence of all that which moves in the world of becoming and, on the other, the indestructible reality of the *I*, of their own deepest Self. Then they reveal the great maxims of the Upanishads to them. And that is all: the spark has made a new lamp to shine. It is the awakening.

The experience of the Mystery in itself transcends the level of what India calls *devas*. The *devas, dii,* or gods, are the diverse manifestations of this mystery, that is to say, ungraspable and impenetrable by thought. They are the divine forces at work in the cosmos, the powers or faculties of the psycho-physiological world at the summit of which is the *deva deva,* the original manifestation of this Mystery. One will call it *Brahma* (personified *Brahman), Ishvara,* the Lord, *Purusha,* as well as diverse names that transmit the traditions of *bhakti* (devotion, devotional love). But for the one who has been marked by the great experience, this *Brahma,* this *Ishvara* are perceived as being the transparency of the Absolute, of the Divine in itself in the phenomenal world. Human thought, of course, will not be able to resist personifying this Mystery or to prevent itself from projecting its own categories onto it so as to be able "to live with it." The *Advaitin* will also freely use this mode of expression in the common language. Nevertheless, in the depth of his being there is an unslakeable thirst, the taste for truth which the experience of this Absolute has deposited in him and which no longer permits him to identify with this Truth in itself anyone of its manifestations. For him it is the marvelous, shimmering *lila* of the Lord which frolics through the worlds.

To be sure this experience of *advaita,* at least in this ultimate point, is the feat only of a tiny select group. The most well-known case in our time is that of Sri Ramana Maharshi of Tiruvannamalai. It would be false, however, to suppose that it exists only in the case of teachers known to the public. It so empties the individual of his or her selfhood that, save for determining circumstances—say, the powerful call of the Spirit—those who have experienced it hardly try to appear or speak in public. It is certain, moreover, that it leads humans into regions of the mental and spiritual life where the air is so rarified that most flinch from it out of fear. Nevertheless it exists among many as an underlying reality. Experienced in its total call by the great *rishis* (seers) of old, it has left its mark on the Scriptures, the cult, the mind and the whole culture of India. Even a Ramanudja, the type of philosopher-theologian who wants at all costs to safeguard in the definitive experience a kind of face to face still of the vision and reciprocal enjoyment of God and of his elect, abstains from touching the fundamental intuition of the *advaita* and, in his symbolic language, affirms merely that the creatures are the cosmic body of the Lord.

The Paths of Experience

The ways of approach to this experience are most often classified in India under three principal titles: *karma, bhakti, jnana.*

The Way of Karma

Etymologically *karma* means: act. The primitive meaning is the cultic act, the act on the religious plane. As in the Jewish Torah, the whole life of the brahman is caught up in the wake of the liturgical act, because nothing in life escapes the divine Omnipresence. A profane order of reality does not exist, everything participates in the sacred. This spiritual path is probably the most ancient that can be identified in India. Its golden age was the so-called period of the Brahmans which immediately followed the Vedic era proper and led to the upanishadic reaction.

Everything, in this world and in the other, depends on the

perfect realization of the cult and on the exact observance of the *shastras* (the laws). The mystic life is rarely discernable therein: it is the primacy of the "sacramental" sign.

The karma of yogic practices and of ascesis, which are also counteractions to the primacy of the cult and the supremacy of the priestly caste, must approximate this ritual karma. One is no longer satisfied with the faith in ritual symbols, one craves to experience the "divine," to live states of ecstasy. And, undeniably the intensive practice of Yoga often leads to such experiences. On the other hand, unquestionably, one still remains on the phenomenal plane and one remains still quite far from the very pure experience of *advaita* described in the Upanishads and mentioned above.

There is also a modern version of the *karma-marga* which unquestionably is rooted in the tradition of India—the Bhagavad-Gita, for example—but which, it seems, also owes much to the impact of the Gospels on the Hindu soul. It is the act in the form of service: *sava,* the karma viewed as service to the human community. It suffices to mention Mahatma Gandhi and his great disciple, Vinoba Bhava. Such a karma, beyond doubt, is eminently tantamount to liberation. For more than any ritual act, and just as any overly defined practice of ascesis, it truly takes man out of himself and out of his instinctive withdrawal within himself, thus rendering him free and totally docile to the inspiration of the Spirit.

The Way of the Bhakti

Bhakti means faith, piety, devotion. It is the Indian spiritual way that comes closest to the Christian spiritual tradition. The *bahkta* (devotee) attaches himself to a personification of the Absolute, such as Shiva, to an *avatara* (an incarnation) such as Rama and Krishna, to the divine Shakti. He serves his God by way of a totally unified thought and volition: meditation, cult, song, *sat-sang* or the company of saints, the service of those who have consecrated themselves to the Lord. As the Bhagavad-Gita, in particular, teaches, there is nothing in the life of the devotee that is not consciously conformed to God and inspired by his love.

Nevertheless, the meditation of the Hindu *bhakta,* rather than being a reflection on the attributes of his God (*Ishta devata*), will prefer much more to behold Him with an ever increasing fixedness, in the course of which the "beholder" progressively disappears in the "beheld." The Lord—Bhagavan responds to the devotion of his *bhakta* with his own love. He bridges the gulf through his grace and finally becomes one with his devotee.

There exist extremely diversified forms of *bhakti,* ranging from the most purified to the most emotional. *Prapatti,* or total self-surrender, is in every way the highest point of *bhakti,* that which gives it its value and supreme efficacy.

At all events, it must not be supposed that the ways of *bhakti* and of *karma* as such are ways of a lower order. Each one has received from God a temperament and a particular grace which determine the path that the person is to follow in this world. When the ways of *bhakti* and *karman* are followed in perfection, they are no less liberative than that of *Jnana,* for their exigencies are no less. It suffices to refer to the classic Bhakti-Sutras of Narada to realize that the way of *bhakti,* in a shrouded form, contains all the essential aspects of *Jnana.*

The Way of Jnana

The way of *Jnana* is that which aims directly at the "Mystery" without concerning itself with its signs or mythic, conceptual, historic, cultural expressions. Jnana is the aristocratic, royal way, if you will; nevertheless, it is not an esoteric way. It vivifyingly permeates all the *margas* (ways). It is preeminently the way of the monk as we shall see later. It has no interest whatsoever in the *devas,* these personifications of the Mystery of the divine power discernible by way of the phenomenal world, the service and love of which would lead him up to the very heavens where they dwell (*svarga*). Nor does it evince any greater interest in either ritual or ascetic practices. Rather, it aims directly at the liberating intuition.

The term *Jnana* means wisdom, knowledge, and too often and wrongly the way of Jnana is interpreted as a way of speculation or of abstraction. It is also improperly compared to these diverse gnosticisms that marked the end of Hellenism and the beginnings of Christianity. *Jnana* does not disclose itself at the end of laborious reflections, nor does it have anything in common with the formulations which, transmitted ritually, would produce the inner illusion as though by magic, for all that remains within the order of the sign. Nevertheless, *Jnana* is an arcane knowledge, a *mysterium fidei,* a mystery of faith to which one can attain only by raising oneself to a higher level of one's consciousness. It is a consciousness that seizes the whole of being and renews it to its very roots.

The way of *Jnana* rejects all signs, also that of a personified God. As useful as it is at the moment of take-off in the spiritual life, the sign itself becomes an obstacle from the moment the devotee *attaches himself* to the image of his God and, by so doing, necessarily re-centers himself upon his own self.

The way of *Jnana* is essentially the way of *dhyana:* that of the meditation of silence. Its aim is to center the consciousness on itself, to prevent it from scattering itself in the world of the image and abstract thought, to lead it back incessantly to the present, even to the here and now and to the very course of all the activities of the mind. It is a matter of awakening to selfhood, beyond all conditioning.

This central point of self can be discovered only by one's self. Even the Scriptures, even the guru can only point out the path, or at best half-open the door of the sanctuary. Naught else but self can penetrate within one's own self. That is why the supreme realization, *brahmavidya,* cannot, strictly speaking, be *attained.* It is there, from the very beginning, it is the very essence of being. *Jnana* is a simple awakening, an illumination of which nothing can be said, except *ASTI:* it is. One opens one's eyes and one beholds the sun that shines on high. The state of *Jnana* is a state of simplicity and total transparence. It is the unborn state: *sahaja,* the inborn self. It is the natural state of man, and his profound truth. It is selfhood in the sense of the *cognitio matutina* of St. Augustine.

Strictly speaking, the way of *Jnana* is not even a way in the sense of Karma or of Bhakti since there actually is nothing to attain or to receive. At best, it is a preparation for this awakening. The awakening, no doubt, can be aided and provoked by a blow, a noise, for example. But is it not the blow or the noise that begets this marvelous a-perception of self in its cosmic environment which is the consciousness of the state of vigil.

Man *is* in time and in the world. His senses are open to what is outside him and he develops mentally only by starting out from successive sensory impressions. He attains to self only in the setting of the cosmos and in human society. Nevertheless, man is an interiority, an *in-Self.* It is this very interiority that gives him his identity and permits him to assimilate the data received from without.

From the moment of the first awakening of his consciousness in the depth of the Universe, man is embarked on a quest of his own self. He seeks himself in the physical and social sciences. But he constantly conjectures something beyond that which his own reflections, as well as the findings of the most advanced psychological techniques, disclose to him concerning selfhood. *Neti, neti,* (No, not this, not that), as the Upanishad proclaims. A chasm, so to speak, separates him from self. Most frequently, man contents himself with myths and formularies, called religions, in order to live this "beyondness" at the level of his thought and of his affectivity. He then calls it God—this God whom he projects beyond himself as though to free himself from this Absolute that suffocates and empties him—the whole domain of the *devas* and of religion. But the moment comes in the history of humankind and, increasingly, in the history of the individual, in which man is obliged to admit that nothing of that which he thinks, feels or experiences is not really self, not really God, not this Absolute. In fact, as long as there is still a self in quest of a self, one has not yet found oneself. Or, rather, when one has discovered that, by virtue of this very discovery one can be said to have attained self-realization, beyond all the changing and successive manifestations of self.

Although man is in time, he is also quite beyond time. The *I* that I pronounce at sixty is in no wise different from the I that I pronounced when I was ten. When man retires within himself and seeks to discover the origin of this *I,* the moment of his awakening to this *I,* however far back it may recede in his memory, there is this *I* who is simply there, the base of all, the source from which all flows but which itself is ungraspable.

The Vedantic meditation aims precisely at the perception of this central point of being, this "immoveable," this *acala* which defies all becoming and remains untouched by any conditioning factor whatsoever.

Man in his phenomenal consciousness perceives himself as one incessantly thinking and acting. The *rishis* of the Upanishads call upon man to perceive himself simply as *being,* to realize this consciousness of absolutely pure being, this infinitesimal point which is at the origin of all consciousness, of all thought, while at the same time transcending all particular thought and the time frame within which it moves. It is the Real, *Sat,* the Self outside of all conditioning of time and thought. It is here alone that man arrives at his inmost truth, he realizes himself in the absolute of his person. What, then, becomes of God?

But here, precisely, is the purest experience of God beyond any *notion* of God. Until then, God was only a notion, a "projection." He was known only in the idea that one had of Him, even if love, in its irresistible elan, went beyond the limits of thought and soared towards Him like a rocket pointed toward outer space. Here one is beyond the *eidos,* the "notion." The Absolute itself has been touched in this experience of the absolute of *Self,* of the *I,* of pure consciousness. But everything of God and of Self has been consumed in the flame of this very experience. The shadow has given way to the Truth. One finally realizes this adoration in spirit and in truth, the primacy of which Jesus came down to earth to recall.

By awakening to self, man has awakened himself to God. By awakening to God, he has awakened himself to self, beyond God and self, in this eternal mystery of the Father, at a point where the Spirit leads this Spirit whom the word of God become man has come to spread all over the world.

Final Summaries

Such is the experience of the divine Mystery which is at the base of the religious experience of the East. It is certainly different from the experience of the prophetic religions, but no less authentic. That the Christian revelation took place in the frame of a prophetic religion, Judaism, is a fact of history and certainly a plan of Providence. Nevertheless Christianity cannot claim a universality which it affirms is inherent to its mystery as long as it has not recognized and integrated this spiritual experience of the East. Moreover, the mystery of Jesus overflows all—the experience called prophetic as well as the experience called Vedantic. But this is not the place to study this necessary osmosis.

It would be worthwhile now to study the means that the Vedic spiritual tradition employs in order to arrive at this awakening. We shall limit ourselves here to some brief remarks since the subject belongs to other papers to be read at this Congress,[4] particularly those that treat of the integration of the ascetic and mystic methods of Hindu and Buddhist monasticism into the Christian monasticism of the East.

Reference was made to these yogic practices whose aim is to produce metaphysical experiences. On the other hand, there is a Yoga, the *Raja-Yoga,* which aims exclusively at preparing this awakening to the pure consciousness of self. They are above all exercises of progressive mental concentration, *dharana,* with some preliminary elements of breath-control, *pranayama,* and stability in posture, *asana.*

Extremely practical methods of concentration have been elaborated in Buddhism. This applies in particular to *Satipathana* and to *Zazen.*

Nevertheless it cannot be forgotten that these methods of concentration begin to come to light only in some relatively late Upanishads. At the level of the great early Upanishads, it seems that the heart and the intelligence of the disciple are so free and open that once the word of truth is proclaimed by the Teacher, the Awakening follows spontaneously in the listener's soul.

In the central monastic tradition of India, the way of *Jnana* is obviously privileged. It suffices to refer to such fundamental texts as the *Samnyas upanishads.* There are, of course, monks of sectarian adherence following the practices of Bhakti, even ritualist monks not to mention those who have chosen the life of *seva-karma* (service to others). That simply attests one more time to the prodigious variety of India's living spiritual tradition.

It seems normal, at all events, that the Christian monks of India let themselves be led by the Spirit towards the complete divestment enjoined by the way of Jnana which corresponds so well to their vocation and prepares the full florescence of all that which is contained in their call. To them, moreover, more than to anyone else in the Christian tradition falls the task of integrating this marvelous richness of the experience of Jnana with the spiritual riches of Christ's faithful, without which the resplendency of the Church cannot be complete.

Chapter 2

India's Contribution

to Christian Prayer[1]

The prayer of the Church is in the process of transformation; the proofs of this are, among others, the new editions of the Roman breviary and missal. Beyond the *devotio moderna,* Christian piety is happily engaged in the process of rediscovering its wellsprings in the Bible and in the thought of the Fathers, in the liturgical expression of the faith of the first Christians, and in the equally rich tradition of the Churches of the Byzantine East. It no longer centers the collects so exclusively on the petition for forgiveness nor on deliverance from dangers, often unnamed. Now it bears much more on faith in the paschal mystery and on the desire to participate in it more completely. It also opens itself to the aspirations of the contemporary world; it tends to discover, though still with some difficulty, in this world that is in the making not so much the slogans that ripple on its surface as those deep aspirations through which the Spirit manifests himself in ever new ways in the depth of the human psyche.

Nevertheless, the ongoing renewal of Christian prayer should go much beyond this point. The Church is *Catholic,* as much as is the faith on which she lives and the Kingdom of God which she proclaims, and also sovereignly free of all conditioning, whether of time or place, race or civilization. The Church is responsible for gathering together the prayer of all humanity in the unique sacrifice of the Lamb, as the seer of *Revelations* prophetically proclaims. In her universal, eschatalogical praise, the Church must embrace all the holy desires formed by the Spirit in the heart of humankind. And already in time, in her march towards the Kingdom to come, the Church must everywhere hearken to the voice of the Spirit who, suffusing everything everywhere, reveals God, proclaims his Christ everywhere and everywhere also addresses himself to his Church.

It is here, it seems, that something is still lacking in the universality of the Church's prayer. To the world of the Spirit it is still like a lunar crescent which rises towards its fullness: now it is only fullness that makes the Church's catholicity visible.

Despite the conciliar and post-conciliar declarations, the Church remains essentially Mediterranean or, if one prefers, Atlantic. And the Christian liturgy will not become catholic, that is to say, *at home everywhere,* merely by simply borrowing some outward gestures from here or there, just as Christian theology will not become catholic merely by making expedient use of concepts gathered or abstracted from the ambient world of ideas. Only an existential penetration of the very sources of the Spirit which abundantly gush forth everywhere will make this development possible. In any event, it is quite certain that in the countries of the Far East, there is a whole part of our soul—the most profound, the most ours, hence the most divine—which does not feel itself to be truly integrated in the official prayer of the Church, not even of the renewed Church. To be sure, the eucharistic prayers, for example, have recovered the best of the great biblical and patristic tradition. Nevertheless, whatever they may be, they remain incapable of expressing the depth of the soul of one who is seeking to celebrate the holy mysteries in connection with all this experience of the Spirit who has prepared here the proclamation of the message of redemption.

Such an expression of the Christian prayer is not only a right belonging to the children of this tradition; even more, it is a right belonging to India as well as to the countries of the

Far East, and it is an inalienable duty of *Catholics* as a whole. The Church and the whole world must open themselves at last to these ultimate depths of the human heart: they belong to each one, to the West as well, even though by the mysterious choice of the Spirit, they have been recognized by the seers of India with an intensity more fulgent than anywhere else. India has the mission to open to man his deepest self, at one and the same time, in *Catholics* and in the world. It is ever more clear today, in fact, that the Church is not *catholic* save in the measure in which the dimensions of her faith and of her experience, of her thought as well as of her prayer, broaden out to become those of the world. In the case that concerns us here, the Church seems to be called to be the providential intermediary between the experience of India and the waiting of the Spirit in the depths of the hearts of the West.

The prayer of India is first of all conspicuously *bhakti,* devotion. The forms of this *bhakti* are multiple, ranging from those of a most discrete to a most passionate character. At times, they even border on aberration. In many ways they often are a blend of those forms of piety observed in the Christian world, eastern and western alike. Nevertheless, there is already in this *bhakti* a freedom that ill-conforms to the classicism and to the measure of Graeco-Latin formulations. The Spirit refuses to be limited in his expression. However, it will not be this freedom of the *bhakti* devotions which will be India's predominant contribution to the prayer of the *Catholic world,* the Church and the world are one and the same time. Africa as well and Latin America can also express the possession of the Spirit in the exuberance of forms and gestures.

The grace proper to India is a call to the profoundest depth of being:

"There from whence words
And mind as well return
After being unable to attain to it."

(Taittiriya-Upanishad)

Such, of course, is the exclusive theme of India's prayer. Yet even behind the exuberances of her *bhakti* there is this *jnana,* this wisdom, this silence, which is characteristic of her faith and her experience of the Beyond. From the outset, the *rishis* of India have been fascinated by this silence of God of the Brahman, the absolute, as the texts say. Penetrating to the depths of his being, man discovers a mystery, which one will call *sien* (supreme), another divine, but which in truth cannot properly be called either *sien* or divine, for these are the words that must be transcended: *That* is beyond all expression, beyond all apprehension alike, whether through the senses or the subtlest intelligence. It is beyond all mental approach: *That is, om tat sat,* simply, *asti,* the *asti* of Horeb, *Iahva* . . . If man as well, attains self-deliverance in this mystery, it is at a depth of the self in which all notions, all that which discloses selfhood to man through reflection and through his phenomenal consciousness, are gone beyond, transcended. Such is the constant theme of the paradoxical instructions and parables of the Upanishads.

A word, or a single syllable, is transmitted by tradition as the privileged means of representing this experience and of leading to it—a sign, to be sure—and which will reveal itself only to the person who has fathomed it beyond the sign. It is the OM (or AUM), the pre-eminent syllable—the *A,* the primordial vowel, clouded over in *O* and prolonging itself in the nasal resonance *M*—the last sound that man is capable of uttering at the moment in which his thought subsides into the essential silence. The texts explain, moreover, that what is most significant about OM is its *fourth quarter* (after a plus u plus m), the total silence, the passage from the brahman pronounced to the brahman ever more un-revealed. The return from it rejoins the beginnings, the essential silence of the brahman from which springs up the manifestation, the abyssal Silence from which proceeds the Word (St. Ignatius of Antioch).

The Christian mystic of the West certainly has also probed the depths of this silence, but Christian tradition has more generally considered that this interior silence could only be received. Even more, it could only be forced, so to speak, by the Spirit on the mind of man. And there is also an anti-mystical current, fortunately in decline, that views this ascendency of the spirit of silence as an anomaly in the spiritual life of the individual, to the point that directors of conscience in India, formed along western lines, at times have forbidden their Christian disciples coming from Hinduism to subside into this silence to which the Spirit quite naturally conveyed them.

It must be stressed here that when India and the great mystical traditions speak of silence, it is not a matter merely of a simple outward silence of the mind. It is the whole mind that observes silence, that rejects any attempt to name The One whom it divines opposite to it, as well as any attempt to express itself, were it even by the most evanescent I, in order to adore, to give thanks, to petition any favor whatsoever. Much more than a rejection, it is an essential incapacity to express in some way this Presence that transcends the mind and immerses it into its primordial abysses. The mystery is then perceived solely in this utter incapacity to fashion a representation, in which the percipient has lost even the consciousness that he perceives.

India has taken with utter seriousness this word that tradition has adopted from Psalm 64: *silentium tibi laus: Thy praise is silence.*

   The Christian of the West and of the East, whom a tem-
porary acculturation has all too often cut off from the well-
springs of his prayer, must re-learn this silence of the soul
before God from eternal India.

   "Oh Thou, the Beyond of All.
   What other name does one have the right to give Thee"

sings Gregory of Nazianzen in his admirable *Hymn to God.*
Nevertheless, as an impenitent Platonist, for ten or fifteen
additional verses, he continues to say to God that He cannot
be uttered, thought or named. The one for whom this silence
of God is no longer an idea, but an annihilating experience, is
no longer able to voice anything whatsoever: Om . . . the eye
that has dared to fix its gaze on the noon-day sun is struck
blind.

   The West would be able to sensitize itself to this mystery
through poetry: a poetry which would recover the intimate
mystery of each thing, even more that of the profoundest
depth of the heart of man, beyond his hopes, his most essential affirmations, at that point where the *I* of man and all that
which manifests him to his own self is still in gestation, so to
speak, a sensitization which could be effected, above all, by
observing silence and by hearkening to the Spirit.

   A proof, among others, that the West, Christian or not, is
engaged in an ardent quest, though unconsciously so at times,
of the experience of silence, is this nostalgia for the Ganges
and the Himalayas that launches so many frustrated young
Europeans or young Americans onto the paths of Katman-
dou or Benares, young people to whom those who should
have been their gurus and spiritual guides have most often
given them only some formulas of prayer and substitutes for
interior life. The modern aspiration is of an existential order,
its slant is towards experience, not ideas, and ultimately

towards the very experience of God, the only experience capable of liberating man and making him flower. To be sure, it is necessary to verify in each case which spirit leads man; nevertheless, no one ever has the right to stifle the Spirit, neither in oneself nor in others. India's spiritual path is wholly marked by this attentiveness to the inner whispering of the Spirit, by this aspiration to total silence.

On the strength of a long tradition and of the ceaselessly renewed experience of the sages, this silence of the mind, paradoxically, is considered as the supreme act of man, as the only expression adequate to the mystery towards which he thrusts, or, rather, in the depth of which he rises outside time. In consequence, far from rejecting or fearing this silence, far even from accepting it passively should it one day force entry into the soul, India teaches her children to prepare themselves directly for this silence. This preparation does not consist, however, in efforts which could not but fail of their purpose, inasmuch as they would be fundamentally opposed to this silence. Rather, it consists of a sort of an increasing de-contraction and relaxation of the tensions and activities of the body and of the mind—all things that are subsumed under the generic heading of yoga. One cannot overly caution against the minimizations of Yoga that at the present time are the fashion in the West, which reduces them to postural and breathing exercises, mixed, among Christians, with pious ejaculations. True Yoga has only one goal: the complete silence of thought, the arrest, as total as possible, of mental movements. The same must be said, moreover, for the Japanese *za-zen* which, at bottom, is but a deviant form of yoga, more easily within reach in consequence of the possibilities obtaining in the western world. But however different its forms, the goal of yoga is always this total silence of the mind, for only in this silence can the unpronounced word of the Spirit—in which God speaks—be heard.

India also has its gurus for teaching one how to climb this path—or, rather, how to plunge into these abysses:

> *"for who would be able to divine that, had he not learned it from another?"*
>
>   (Katha-Upanishad)

But this teaching is a communication of experience, not a simple transmission of thought through words. As real *gurus* rarely have a house of their own, an encounter with them is a pure act of grace.

There are also the Scriptures and the writings of the saints. But here still, without initiation by a teacher, who would know how to discover the hidden marrow? Nevertheless, when the soul is already opened from within, reading these Scriptures in the spirit of faith is bound to engender in the soul increasingly deep resonances until the day when the inner enlightenment will bear the soul upwards toward its most real *self*. Thus, this reading can also be a point of departure, and it would be eminently desirable if the Western Christian also habituates himself to prayerfully read the most beautiful of these texts, either in the privacy of his or her dwelling, or even in an ecclesial gathering for they, too, contain a message of the Spirit.

For the Christian, this prayer of silence must first of all be the ideal of his relationship to God. He will rise to it no doubt by degrees, in the measure in which the Spirit liberates him from his overly great need for mental activity. There is, of course, a great number of different temperaments and individual charisms. There are ages in the spiritual life and each one, moreover, has his or her personal vocation which it would be sacrilegious not to respect. Nevertheless, even among those who do not seem to be called immediately to that inner silence, it is of surface importance that they at least be initiated to the call of the Spirit within, to this sense of interiority which will help them to collect their thoughts, progressively liberate them from the congenital dispersion of their mind, and will animate the most formulated of their prayers and, finally, little by little, will make them penetrate into the *holy of holies:*

> *"This inmost center*
> *this sky higher than all skies,*
> *the abode of the Brahman."*

(Taittiriya-Upanishad)

Furthermore, only when the soul actually penetrates into this holy of holies will it free itself from this conception of *interiority* which doubtless will have helped it in its progress but which one day risks limiting it. For at the profoundest depth of the inwardness, there no longer exists a within or without but only the uncircumscribable ocean of the unique Mystery, present everywhere, everywhere in Self, radiant in all with its particular and infinite light.

The antinomy that in our day poses itself so harshly on the Christian consciousness will likewise be resolved at this summit: namely, that of the sacred and the profane and also that of theological and religious pluralism. In short, the antinomy of the cosmic Christ, the Pancreator, and of the Christ of the biblical revelation. As long as God—or the Mystery—is led back to the name that a group of humans give to Him or to the notion of Him fashioned by them, as long as His unnameableness is still a concept, an idea—the apophatism of theology—it is quite difficult for the believer—without staking the value of the expression of his faith—to recognize everywhere the total mystery of this Presence. Only when the soul has undergone the experience that the Name beyond all names can be pronounced only in the silence of the Spirit, does one become capable of this total openness which permits one to perceive the Mystery in its sign—in all the forms of the sacred and the profane—in the sign that reveals all and that, at the same time, points always towards the Beyond. Is not the Kingdom proclaimed by the Gospel, the pre-eminent sign of this Presence, always and essentially a thing in the offing? Up to the last day the Church will pray: "Thy Kingdom come."

And if some persons are troubled because they are no longer able thus to name God in their prayers, if they believe that God escapes them once they can no longer *think* Him, should this not be attributed, rather, to their fear of escaping from themselves, as though outside this God of their conception, they might lose their identity? The prohibition of images that God enjoined on Mount Sinai and which Deuteronomy repeats so forcibly goes well beyond images engraved on stone or wood. Let those who still doubt meditate on the Scriptures and, above all, remain in silence hearkening to the Spirit.

This sense, or this experience of the Presence beyond all names will permit one to recognize the Presence everywhere, in each being and in each happening. And that, too, will be a gift of India to Christian prayer. To be sure Christian faith from the outset was marked by the revelation of God through the events unfolding in history. But it is precisely this attention to history and to the paschal act that consummates it which has often prevented the Christian from recognizing in its full value the presence of God in the world, His cosmic revelation. By evacuating the gods of the classic mythologies, the biblical revelation separated God from his creation for many believers,

> *"Heaven belongs to Yahweh,*
> *Earth he bestows on man"*

(Ps. 115)

whereas, despite the danger of pantheism (actually often more verbal than real) India, for example, remains fascinated by this Presence, penetrating and overhanging at one and the same time, a Presence that is anterior to the wholly human distinction between the sacred and the profane. For is there anything whatsoever in which the totality of the mystery of the Brahman does not shine?

Silence and Presence, silence that is presence and presence that is silence, such is essentially the call of the Spirit to the Christian in prayer, through the agency of India.

But it is clear that this prayer of silence and presence cannot be limited to some moments of the day or of life. There are, of course, high points when man recalls the mystery or re-enters more consciously into this inwardness. But all of life is marked by this essential attitude. Even these high points have no other aim than that of deepening an experience that never ceases.

These high points, first and foremost, must be consecrated to this self-communion every day and, for as long a time as possible, morning and night. They should also be several minutes of great and deep silence at different moments of the day. The Indian practice of *japa*—the repetition of the divine name—so close to the Graeco-Russian tradition of the Jesus Prayer—is also an excellent auxiliary, especially if it is said on the aforementioned *OM* and on the natural rhythm of the heart beats or of respiration.

This prayer of silence will happily underlie all ecclesial prayer. After all, is not all communitarian prayer ecclesial prayer? Is not Christ there, and his Spirit, and his Church, everywhere where two or three of his own "meet in his name" as the Gospel says? And who then can be said to be outside the mystery of Christ and of his Spirit? In the final analysis there are communitarian prayers which can be nothing else but prayers of silence, when the fundamental difference in "forms" no longer allows for a common word so that the Mystery can be recited together. This silent communion in the depth is no less close, even the closest of all, when each one of the participants has attained to "this deepest center" in himself or herself. Such is also the most essential dimension of all genuine dialogue, for genuine dialogue can be nothing else but prayer, communication in the Spirit.

Could one conceive, finally, that this prayer of total inner silence has its place in the liturgy properly so-called? That the periods of silence now being called for in the celebration of liturgy play the role of the last quarter of *OM* in the Hindu tradition, that is to say, that all expressed prayer finds in this silence its origin and its completion at one and the same time? One dreams of contemplative communities in which the hearing of the Word is lost in this silence and in which the eucharistic prayer that follows it consists only of some pregnant words, weighty with meaning, at the outermost limit of expression, gushing forth from this silence.

One would like also to hope that, in the upcoming legislation, the rights of the prayer of silence will be recognized for the contemplative religious when he or she, in the privacy of the cell, performs the duty of ecclesial prayer. Neither the psalms, nor even less the most recent hymns, can express the prayer of the Christian in each hour of his or her life, above all of one who has been initiated to the prayer of silence by the Spirit. In the manner of the Greek monk, who is still authorized, whenever the need arises, to replace the hours of his office by the repetition of the Jesus Prayer, why could not the Christian contemplative substitute the psalms and hymns of his or her liturgical books by the murmur of *OM*, for example, if he or she belongs to the Indian tradition, or even if the Spirit impels him or her to do this, by the simple inward gaze beyond any formulation? The Benedictine tradition calls the Divine Office the work of God, *opus Dei*. Does not God, therefore, work when He expresses himself from without? Even more, could it not be said that His *opus* springs from his *otium*, this sabbath into which He re-entered on the seventh day. Happy is he who has entered the sabbath of God, as says the author of the Epistle to the Hebrews.

Great indeed is the predestination of India through whose voice the Spirit is engaged in recalling to the Church the primacy of the *Sabbath of God.*

Chapter 3

The Theology of Presence
As a Form of Evangelization
In the Context of Non-Christian Religions[1]

The notion of "presence" has become a *leitmotif* of missionary literature. At times "the apostolate of Presence"—as it is called—is considered as underlying the totality of the process of evangelization; other times it is understood as a special form of evangelization, distinct from direct preaching, from dialogue, and from the work of development; and at times it is even viewed as a form of preparation in places where circumstances do not yet permit other missionary approaches. This study will deal with the theological foundations of the notion of Presence in the mission of the Church and try to glean from it the implications for evangelization on the whole.

I. Theology

Philosophical Bases

Existential analysis shows that the notion of Presence simultaneously involves consciousness of self and relationship with others or, more precisely, it means the integration of our relationship with others with self-consciousness. This means that acceptance of the fact of "being with others" is not something peripheral in the consciousness, corresponding only to a superficial level of consciousness, but that this relationship is experienced at the very depth in which one is one's own self, that is to say, in which one is eminently conscious of one's selfhood. The immediate consequence of this is that the only person who is capable of communicating with others at this profoundest depth of their being is the one who himself has had the experience of pure consciousness of self, as Vedantic tradition puts it.

Given that presence signifies reciprocity or, at least, the possibility of reciprocity of consciousness, of being present to other human beings, and this is involved in "being present in the world," it does not simply mean taking an interest in others, or being serviceable to them when the opportunity arises. Rather, it means being concerned for them in the compass of the interest that I entertain towards myself, on the temporal and escatalogical level alike. It is an ontological attitude of service, of being "for others," *ad alios*. It is what in evangelical terms is called love, a love that leads even up to the gift of one's life if circumstances so require. Moreover, it is not a love that can be limited to someone of my choice. I must be ready to live this I-Thou relationship up to its last implications with no matter what human being whose path crosses mine.

Biblical Covenant

The mystery of the Presence, otherwise called the I-Thou relationship underlies the whole biblical Revelation. Even in Eden, Adam lived an I-Thou relationship with God. After Noah and Abraham, the Old Testament unbrokenly highlights the notion of "Covenant," something that goes very much farther than the simple dependance of the creature vis-a-vis his Creator, and which leads up to the "face to face" of Moses with Yahweh. The Covenant pact revealed in the Bible is taken so seriously by God that when it is broken by man, He sets about doing everything to lead man back to

Him and to renew the intimacy. Finally, God sends His Son
to the earth, and even onto the Cross, in order to restore the
Covenant.

Creation, redemption and incarnation are, in their inward
essence, a mystery of the reciprocal presence between man
and God, in short: the mystery of love.

Interior Life of God

Only with difficulty could it have been otherwise since the
creation—taken in its full space-time relations—is the
manifestation of the very mystery of God on the level of time
and becoming, and since man has been created in "the image
and likeness of God" as the Scriptures say. Revelation
teaches us that the divine Life is in itself a mystery of
Presence. God exists in three Persons, as theology asserts.
The first Person is only in the generation of the Son and the
second Person is only in the eternal generation of the Father;
the final mystery of the Spirit is the consummation in the
non-duality, *advaita,* of the I-Thou of the Father and of the
Son. It is in this eminently divine I-Thou (including its own
consummation in the *advaita* of the Spirit) in which man participates in his self-awareness which he lives outwardly with
others under the sign of his I-Thou relationship with them.

The fact of having originated in the creation and in the free
will of God does not render the relationship between man and
God any less intimate and does not prevent it from rising
from the very center and the inward being, at one and the
same time, of man and God. Although the Bible presents
God to us in his inaccessible glory, it no less affirms the *ad
hominem* of the interior life of God.

II. Christology

Manifestation of Christ

Jesus Christ is the authentic manifestation on earth of the divine mystery of Presence, He himself being in his own Person the eternal Presence of the Father to himself. He was born among men in order to teach them the plenitude of this mystery and to rescue them from the bondage of sin for which very reason they reject this Presence either in their own selves or in regard to their fellow human beings.

Jesus, however, does not contribute any theory to the subject of God or of man. He simply shows an example and a way to men: in their name he lives up to the end—*usque ad finem*—that is to say, up to the cross and death—all and everything that involves an authentic presence to God and to his brothers in the profoundest depth of his being. Voluntarily, He lived among men his own experience of being an I-Thou with the Father and with each one among them. By acting thus, He revealed to man the depth of his own I-Thou with God, man's own condition of also being "born of God," like Him.

Jesus taught his disciples to love God with all their heart, that is to say, without any restrictions whatsoever and with no backsliding to a concern with their own selves, to be docile to His Spirit and attentive to His Will, to prefer that will to their own, even unto death if need be. The fact is that God is and remains invisible and that even the eminently perfect sign of God that was Christ was not to remain forever perceptible to human vision: whence the second commandment through which alone the first can be put into practice. The mystery of the presence of man to God and to Christ must be lived through the concrete presence of each and every human being to each and every other. For us the experience of Christ and of the Trinity consists in the fact that anyone among my fellow humans is "closer to myself than myself" (*intimior intimo meo*), more interior to me one could say than my own interiority to my own self. This signifies a presence which envelops and penetrates my life in its totality, entirely like the presence of the Father to Jesus, the true Son of God and the true Son of Man.

Living his experience of the Presence up to its ultimate consequences which stripped him of his own self, Jesus saved man from his congenital selfishness. In his physical death, he realized the supreme gift for the Redemption of humanity. In his Resurrection, he relinquished all the particularities of his human Incarnation in order to be simply the Man, the *Purusha,* in Indian terms, that is to say, The One who is present to all, living in all, free of any particularized form and of any limit imposed by the categories of time and space. The only cult that he required of his disciples consisted in the re-actualization of the sacred Supper that he celebrated with them on the eve of his death and in which all participated in his *delivered* body, in his *shed* blood, and in which no one can honestly participate if, in the depths of one's heart, one is not *delivered* to all: ready to be the *nourishment* of all and to shed one's blood for anyone whomsoever, thus participating in the essential sacrifice of Christ.

Cosmic Presence of Christ

From the outset, Christian reflection was conscious of the fact that the mystery of Christ could not be narrowly limited to the mortal life of Jesus of Nazareth, nor even to his perpetual life in the heart of the faith of his disciples. Inasmuch as Christ is forever living after his Resurrection, he must have existed prior to his human manifestation. Nevertheless, the pre-existence of Christ cannot be restricted to his divine nature abstractly conceived and bearing no relation to the created world. It must be recognized in the very history of man acceding progressively to his selfhood. Even the divine generation of Christ was not revealed to man independently of his birth as the Son of Man. Nor could the I-Thou of the inner life of God be thought or contemplated save by starting out from the experience of the human presence of human beings among themselves. This is what led the Church Fathers to see in the theophanies of the Old Testament several manifestations of The One who was to incarnate himself at the advent of the fullness of time.

There is truly no reason whatsoever to limit the manifestation of the mystery of Christ to the direct preparations of the Incarnation which constitute the subject of biblical history. We certainly have the right to believe that in any individual who awakens to the divine Presence—it matters not under what symbols it is apprehended—there is already an unveiling of the mystery of Christ, that is to say, a "revelation" to man of the Presence of God to his self. Taken in all its amplitude, the mystery of Christ is in fact this awakening of the Son to the Father in the heart of men, and in the bosom of all creation. Even if the formulations of the Religions of the cosmic Covenant may seem strange to those who have grown up too exclusively in the Semitic or Hellenic tradition, there is none among them that does not testify to the unfolding of the mystery of Christ among men and throughout their history.

Limiting ourselves here to the Hindu tradition, the *Purusha*[1] of the *Vedas* and of the *Upanishads* and the *Sat-Guru*[2] of the later epochs, for example, are nothing less than special approaches of the theandric mystery. The mystery of Christ is also indubitably present and living in the *bhakti*[3] which delivers the devotee of all concern regarding his person and from all attachments to his selfhood, and which transforms his whole thought and his entire life into a simple gaze of love fixed upon the Beloved, thus stripping him, so to speak, of his own self conceived as "separate." Even more mysteriously, but no less revealing of the Spirit, is the experience of the depths of being in which man is almost incapable of recovering his proper place in the bosom of the essential I-Thou of Being, so greatly has his mind been completely "silenced" by the intensity of the Presence. For reasons of space we can only mention here the intense desire of Hindus for the experience of the Presence in the depth of the heart of man as well as in the entire universe. The soul that has immersed itself sufficiently into itself and into the heart of Christ cannot fail to recognize in all this the work of the Spirit.

Here, without wishing to ignore completely the movements of post-Christian western humanism, could not one suggest that it is precisely this mysterious experience of the Presence that is trying to emerge and to express itself in a new way, for example, in the present-day quest for a greater social justice and a more universal brotherhood among all members of the human race? They may openly reject the Name that the religious have given to God or to Christ but, nevertheless, is it not their divine I-Thou which is often authentically lived under the sign of brotherly love, and which, at times, leads them to suffering, torture and even to death?

III. Ecclesiology

The Church

In the wake of the manifestation of Christ in the evangelical context, the Spirit erected the Church in the world as the sign and sacrament of his perpetual and universal Presence. The Church is the unfolding within time and up to the farthest ends of the earth of the theandric mystery which is Christ. The Church is the *gathering* of all those who have realized in Jesus their I-Thou with God and with their fellow human beings. The function of the Church is to propagate the awakening of his Presence among men. The local assemblies of believers are the manifestation in the frame of different cultures, times and places, of this *communion* or *koinonia* of the Spirit, the particularized expressions of the correlative Presence of the Father and of the Son lived in fraternal community among men.

This awakening is indefinitely spread by the very strength of the Spirit because no man really awakened, by virtue of the very fact of his awakening, can do anything else but spontaneously draw others out of their slumber. The communion of believers is an open fraternity: the very moment in which it closes itself off and curls in on itself, it transforms itself into a sect and ceases to be Christian, and "catholic" even less. The fraternity of Christ embraces all peoples, its call is launched to all, its sign is Love, and Love is the gift of one's self without measure.

The Task of the Church

It is clear that the Church's principal task in regard to humanity consists in bringing to full blossom these buds of the experience of the Presence such as they are found in the heart of every sincere person, to awaken in plenitude each one to one's own self and to make one live "to the very end" one's theandric relationship of love with God and others.

The Church cannot avoid taking the form of a human organization since man is a social being. Nevertheless, the variety of fundamental ecclesiologies, as is found in the New Testament, is the guarantee of the Church's ability to adapt herself to whatsoever sociological situation that could arise in the course of time. It is also necessary for the Church to incarnate her profound experience of faith in formulas, since man lives in a world of "mental signs." Nevertheless, the very depth of the Church's experience is such that it can be expressed in several ways in relation to the particular genius of different cultures. On the other hand, however, no particular theology will ever be able to exhaust the plenitude of what the Church contains. But before all else, this signifies that the Church is primordially—beyond her manifestation on the mental and sociological planes—the very mystery of the Presence, lived among men gathered in the *koinonia* (communion) of the Spirit. Her veritable reason for being is to awaken them to it. The aim of evangelization is not, in the first place, to bind the peoples to a visible institution through which the communion of the Spirit is manifested socially, nor to make them accept the words and the notions through which a given tradition has formulated the experience of the Father that was made by Jesus Christ and such as it was shared by the apostles. Rather, the aim is to disclose in their hearts this experience of the divine I-Thou which is there waiting to be revealed, and to make it fully and really present to themselves, to God and to their fellow human beings.

The bond to the Church will be merely a consequence, the result of this awakening to God and to self or "interior conversion." That will occur spontaneously and immediately when the Church is recognized manifestly as the incarnation of this *koinonia* and of this Presence.

It is clear that this mission of the Church to *awaken* goes well beyond the compass of her members or of her future converts. The Church is responsible for all before God, since the call of the Spirit is addressed to all. The Church's vocation carries her beyond the possibilities that she herself may have for preaching the coming of the Kingdom or for distributing the sacraments. This obliges the Church to discover ever new ways for being present in all in the Spriit, and for awakening all human beings to the saving Presence, even if these new ways are apparently not of any outward benefit to her, that is to say, even if they do not signify an increase in membership in the Church or a reinforcement of her reputation in the eyes of the world. Finally, the Church's task is merely to be the leaven which, spread throughout the dough, causes it to rise, even at the risk, at the extreme limit, of having to lose her individual appearance in the course of the process.

Res et Sacramentum

The Church is a sacrament, as Vatican Council II has formulated it: *sacramentum visibile hujus salutiferae unitatis* (LG9). Every sacrament conforms to its *res* (the reality that it signifies and towards which it wishes to lead), and this is equally true for every ministry, whether it is consecrated to the cult or to preaching. The *res* must never be lost from sight. The sacraments must reflect the splendor of the *res* which they conceal and make it manifest in broad daylight. This is all the more urgent in this particular moment of history in which everywhere—within Christianity and Hinduism alike, for example—the traditional forms and the *mythoi* (myths) are being rejected by blaming them for being more of an obstacle than a help in the experience of the Real.

The era of the myths and of the *devas*[1]—or of religion, as many would like to say—is over. The teaching of the Church no longer impresses; her cult, even if renewed, too often fails to touch people to the depths of their being. In the East, on account of these recent efforts, everything that the Church brings is inextricably tied to a particular type of culture and mental background so that only very rarely does the Church reach the heart's core of Eastern man. Most of her present-day adaptations and reformulations disappoint all hopes because they remain at that level that is called religious; obviously, they do not spring up from the inner experience, the *res* of any *sacramentum*. In India particularly, so long as the

Hindu's intense and deep craving for the experience of Presence and its realization will not have been found by the Church in her own depths, all attempts at a new theology and liturgy are foredoomed to failure.

The dissatisfied Hindus in India, like all the dissatisfied of the whole world, will address themselves to the ministers of the Church in order to ask them for the secret of peace and of the true way only when it will become manifest, beyond the forms and the rites, that the Church's primordial intention is to lead men and women to this inner experience of Presence.

Temporal Task

As much as the Church must be present to all, so must she also be present to *each* individual. This means that the Church cannot escape the obligation of being also concerned about the temporal needs of human beings, above all of the most needy among them under the penalty of directly denying the most immediate implications of this mystery of Presence of which she is the bearer in this world. The greatest number of people live in a state of deep misery, physical or moral; what they primarily require in order to become capable of awakening to their own selves is the interest and the loving attention of those who are already thus awakened and who, therefore, are able to look upon them with true loving kindness. To the extent that it is effected in a really disinterested way, this will be the first revelation of Presence for these people.

This does not imply, however, that the Church authorities as such must take all the initiative to attend to such needs by launching or maintaining *ad hoc* church institutions. It is in the first place up to each Christian to be concerned to the depths of his being with such needs and to do everything possible in the measure of his own personal capacities and according to the demands of his surroundings. Next, in concert with other Christians, he must be a "leaven" or the "salt" in organisms which have been set up for this purpose by public or private initiative and, if necessary, start such organisms but outside of any sectarianism. All this work of Christians will be aroused and inspired from within by their sense of duty in this regard—or rather, because they are moved by this impulse that drives them to be present to all and everybody, as was mentioned earlier. They will never forget that, if an adequate organization and administration are indispensable for material efficiency, loving attention and personal contact are even more important for transmission to the poor of the joy that they desire above all else. The special role of the Church's ministers in everything connected with the development and promotion of material good things is to arouse this consciousness among Christians and to make them realize all the implications of their confession of faith in Christ.

Dialogue

Even more than to man's temporal needs, the Church must be present to his spiritual aspirations and desires. This means that the Church must listen and even hear in her own heart the call to God that arises from the depth of all sincere souls. Therefore, the Church must be *present* to all in the midst of the different cultures and religions through which this call is expressed and find in them at least a beginning of change.

The Church must engage in the dialogue of salvation with every human being and do this by taking account of the preparations and the personal vocations proper to each one. Many phases and forms are possible for such dialogue; but any dialogue that purposes to be valid and authentic must dig its roots in a profound awareness of Presence. There can be no genuine communication between human beings which is not first of all communion in the Spirit at the deep level of "heart." There really is no other way beside this for the purpose of understanding and encountering the "inner man" beyond the appearances that, at one and the same time, hide and disclose him.

Dialogue as Presence means exchange, that is to say, the art of giving and of receiving. Receiving is first of all giving of oneself; and that goes very much further than the gift of that which one possesses. This is why the dialogue conducts the Church to a *kenosis* (a divestment) and makes her ever more similar to the resurrected Christ, thus preparing her for the free and plenary manifestation of the Spirit in the universe.

Vocation to Contemplation

Whatever point of view one assumes, it appears that the essential mission of the Church is that of awakening human beings to the unique Presence and of making them ever more present to God and to their fellow creatures. But nobody can awaken another if he or she himself or herself is not fully awakened. Whence the fundamental duty of the Church to "remain awakened," "vigilant" as the Lord has said—and to be increasingly intensely conscious of the Presence that she herself is: only then will the Church be able to be present to the world and to each individual in the manner that she is enjoined to do this by the Spirit. In other words, this means that "contemplation" must be accorded primacy in the Church.

By contemplation we wish to signify this experience of deep consciousness of self to which we have repeatedly referred earlier. This has nothing to do with such notions as withdrawal from the world or flight to the desert. Even less has it to do with the will to keep the mind far from the concerns of the City of Man so that one would be able freely to enjoy an abstract and self-styled spiritual world—in reality, an altogether human fabrication—a temptation that has always been strong among Christians and Hindus alike. On the contrary, when the awakening to the Spirit occurs, at the very center of the soul all distinctions are transcended and it is no longer possible for anything to hide the universal Presence of this very Spirit nor to dissimulate the call sent out from the Spirit to each and every individual in the actual circumstances of his or her own existence.

Nevertheless, the call to the desert is not a myth, and the Church must accept and respect such a-cosmic vocations which, better than any other, can render her present beyond all signs in the very heart of humanity and of each human being. But even more than these charismatic vocations which ought rather be left to the sole discretion of the Spirit, the Church must take special care of the call to contemplation that is inscribed in everyone's heart, by encouraging and nourishing it.

The Church must see to it that all spiritual formation—and, in consequence, all pastoral and theological formation—lead to a desire for such experience and conduct individuals up to the crucial point where the Spirit can engulf them in the inmost core of the ineffable I-Thou relationship of the Father and of the Son.

Ministry of the Presence

The essential ministry in the Church is, consequently, the ministry of Presence. All the ministries are rooted in Christ, conformed to Him, and receive their value and their plenary efficacy from Him. In this age of secularization, there is a great temptation for the ministers of the Church to emulate lay persons and thereby give priority to worldly matters such as economic and political problems. However, they have been ordained for a specific spiritual ministry. In India, for example, Christian priests may not try either to become a kind of pundit or priests attached to the temple, nor may they compete with the technicians of all kinds who work on developmental projects. However, they may choose to be, in the manner of the *sannyasis* ("renouncing" monks) of earlier times and of today, the manifest sign among men of the Presence of the Spirit in the world.

This does not mean to say that they necessarily must lead an a-cosmic life; any honest career whatsoever can be suitable to them, secular or "ecclesiastic." Nevertheless, wherever they may find themselves, before all else they must be at the service of all their brothers and sisters in need of spiritual light whether they be Hindus, Christians, Moslems, Buddhists, indeed even atheists. They must be such as to be immediately recognizable as *gurus*—that is to say, as awakened human beings and, consequently, able to awaken others in turn. Now more than ever, the Christian ministry must aim at the *res* and not content itself with furnishing people mental signs, as glorious as they may be. It can no longer limit itself to those who have already confessed the sovereignty of Christ or who are capable of recognizing it one day. The ministry of the Church is universal and cosmic as is the ministry of Christ himself, priest of the order of Melchisedech, the cosmic priest by definition.

The whole of missionary work consists in placing man face to face with God by placing him face to face with Christ. That happens when a non-believer, upon meeting a Christian, recognizes in him or her the radiance of what we have called the I-Thou of the correlative Presence of the Father and of the Son.

What the world needs most at the present time are persons who have met God in Christ and who bear witness to Him with the spontaneity and the freedom of a John or a Paul. To evangelize means to lead each human being to a personal encounter with Jesus, and then to allow the Spirit of Jesus to act freely in the mind and in the heart of this man or this woman, and manifest his Presence in the manner that he will choose. Nobody, however, can make known the Presence of Jesus, if

Jesus is not already a living presence for him or for her.

This is why it is impossible to believe that this Presence is only one form among others of evangelical work, or still less a single preparation for dialogue or for direct preaching. There is no genuine evangelization that is not essentially communication of the unique Presence through the total presence to one's fellow-creature on the part of the bearer of the message of Christ. As the Gospel says, Christ has come to earth so that men may have life; and the only genuine way—that which never ends—is that of knowing the Father and of being known by Him, in the bosom of the eternal I-Thou of the only begotten Son, in the unity of the Spirit.

Chapter 4

India and the Carmelite Order[1]

The Lord God set up his Church as a sign among the nations (Is. 11, 10, 49, 22), as a standard lifted above the time and space of the universe so that in the Church and through the Church the multitude of the dispersed of Israel might everywhere assemble to the glory of the Holy One.

The mission of the Church is to proclaim to all and everywhere the call of the Risen Jesus and to make disciples of all the nations (Matt. 28,19). And the final aim of the mission is the "recapitulation" (Eph. 1,10) of everything in the Church so that in the fullness of time and of the mystery of God (Rev. 10, 6-7) everything is brought back to the Father so that "God may be all in all (1 Cor. 15,28).

It is through the Church that the prophesy of the Lord, in chapter 12, verse 32 of St. John, is realized: "And when I am lifted up from the earth, I shall draw all men to myself." Nothing can remain outside, neither of Christ nor of the Church, for in the Word all comes from God, all goes to God, and the Church is the body and the plenitude (Eph. 1,23) on earth of the Word become flesh. Time is nothing else but the realization of the plan of the advent of what is eternally true, the passage (Jn. 13,1) of Jesus in his "Body" to the glory that is his from before the beginning of time (Jn. 17,5).

The Church, the sign among all nations, is for this reason priest among them, exercising in them in time the eternal and royal priesthood of Jesus Christ.

The role of the priest is to do homage for all and everyone, of everything brought on the altar of the Most High and transformed, according to the biblical expression, into a sacrifice of a fragrance agreeable to His Majesty.

As Isaiah says (Chap. 60), this fragrance is first of all the wealth of nations and, therefore, firstly their spiritual treasures which thus rise and are consecrated on the altar of Yahweh in his Temple of the new Zion.

The entire universe must be consecrated to the Lord, all must be "sanctified" (cf. Jn. 17, 17-19). The Eucharist is its sign, annunciation, call and eschatological realization of all together under the veil of the sacrament. The Church draws all to herself from the very *breathing* of the Spirit that abides in her, and from her consecrated being she consecrates all: the Church is essentially "eucharist." In a way the Church is the assumption and the transubstantiation to her—and through her to the Lamb, her Spouse—of all the values borne by the universe. The Church is the leaven which, little by little, penetrates the paste and transforms it totally (Matt. 13,33).

The Church is at once the expansion and the gathering of the Kingdom, its "collectedness" in the final consummation.

If in effect, all that possesses being bears of necessity, the trinitarian mark, this must be verified, more than anywhere else, in the Church, the summit of the creation and the culmination of the work of God. Now in the divine mystery, in the mystery of Being, there exists what theologians call a double procession: that which manifests itself through the face to face of the Father and of the Son, then, in and through the Son, through the call to being and to the divine filiation of all that which exists on earth and in the heavens—that which is manifested in the collectedness in the bosom of the Father, of the Son and of all in the Son, in the Spirit of oneness.

If the Church, in the mystery of the Word, is communication and propagation of the Word in the mystery of the Spirit, is it not "collectedness" and return to the Father of all that which, in this Word, has received communication of being, of life, and of truth?

The mission and the assumption are no more distinct in the Church than are the Word and the Spirit in God. The nature of God is to be the Only One and everything that participates in God participates in his essential mystery of oneness, of *a-dvaita*² or non duality, as India expresses it.

I

The Church therefore is the gathering in Christ for God of the peoples of all times and races, along with the treasures that were dealt out by divine Providence, individually as well as collectively, in their eternal predestination.

As Jesus makes us understand in the Gospel, to some God gave one talent, to others ten, but no one was sent away empty-handed. But some, more than others, cooperated with grace and further fructified the talents that were entrusted to them.

When the time was fulfilled God sent his Son to collect and gather these treasures. The Son came to earth at the place and time chosen by the Father. He lived among his own and his own, on the whole, neither recognized him nor received him. But to those who did receive him, he entrusted the mission of spreading themselves everywhere on the earth in order to gather the harvest prepared by the Spirit: this was the Church.

India, like every people, received her store from God. Some, perhaps, will say that the child of India tends to overestimate the riches of his heritage. Nevertheless, who could deny that the encounter of India and the Church does not have an historical parallel with the encounter of the Church and the Hellenic world at the very beginnings of her growth on the earth?

However, when the Gospel came into contact with Hellenic

civilization the latter was in full flower. At that time the civilization of India also was shining in all its brilliance and spreading itself throughout southeastern Asia in the same manner with which Greece, for its part, had inundated the whole Mediterranean basin. Its first Scriptures had already at that time pre-dated by centuries those of the sages of Greece as well as those of the prophets of Israel. At the very time of the advent of the Savior India breathed out from her heart this unmatched poem of divine love, the *Song of the Lord* or Bhagavad-Gita. The great theologians of India were the contemporaries of the Church Fathers and of the doctor of the high Middle Ages. However, in accordance with God's secret plans, the hour of the great encounter with Christ had not yet struck for India.

At the hour when, finally, the Church truly encountered India, India had unfortunately lost much of her glory. Centuries of foreign domination stifled her rise and did not allow for the normal development of her riches. Now India is threatened by the general drift of the world towards an a-religious humanism. Also many of those who behold India from the outside, and even a growing number of India's own children, poorly distinguish the secret of the grace that the Spirit, so preciously, has hidden in her heart.

Nevertheless, ignored or recognized, India's secret is there, ever alive, ever ardent, ever offered to the individual who opens his or her eyes to the self within,[3] to the individual whose soul is attuned to the interior mystery. For that is the veritable secret of India, it is in the depth of one's own soul that it will finally be discovered by the individual who will have been wise enough to go seek it there.

At the heart of the Church and at the heart of India, at one and the same time, God waits for his Church to arrive to disclose this secret of India.

God is patient. He waits and will wait as long as necessary. So long as his Church is not ready to immerse herself "in the profoundest depths" and there gather this pearl, He will continue to inspire the sages of India. He will maintain unbroken the line of the *rishis,* the depositaries and guardians of this secret, visibly and manifestly outside this indifferent Church, but invisibly and in reality, lying in her very bosom in a long gestation.

To discover this pearl one in effect must accept to dive into this depth, and very deeply—immersing oneself in it as far as the very loss of self in self, as far as the "trespass" of self. To plunge to the depth of India's spiritual existence: that is where her Scriptures and the unbroken tradition of the great mystics invite us. We must also plunge into the experience of Christian faith down to its profoundest depths where, for example, we find John and Paul—eminently befitting models and precursors and, after them, a host of ever-living witnesses.

It must not be an intellectual immersion which in reality reveals so little, even less an immersion by way of the imagination or of affectivity, which are even more futile. Rather, it must be a plunge to the well-springs of being, in the place where India awaits, in the place where the Church awaits—where India waits for her secret to be disclosed in and by the Church, where the Church waits for India to disclose from her depths the most precious pearl perhaps that ever adorned her diadem.

In reality it is the Church who waits in the depths of India's heart: the Church who of herself, to be sure, is transcendent over time and place but who reveals herself in the diversity of times and places, the eschatological Church, the Church of India in the mind of God, beautiful with an irreplaceable beauty, the Church which, in the mystery of God, is one with the Spirit and which, with the Spirit, cries out: *veni Domine,* come Lord, and take possession of these riches that are Thine, of this glory that is Thine, that was destined for Thee before the beginning in the predilection of God.

India also waits, united in the plans of God with this Church in whom she was elected and whom she must herself become in time: Christian India, as though groaning in a long and painful parturition. Hindu India likewise waits. To be sure she does not wait with a clear and outer consciousness for she does not yet *know*. Rather, she awaits at a very profound level, in the recesses of her heart, deeper than any consciousness. Hindu India, which cannot but feel how crucial for her is the present *kairos,* the opportune hour, awaits as though weeping in the Spirit in the face of the materialism and religious indifference that are undermining her and demanding to be finally relieved of her centuries-old guard: *custos, quid de nocte:* "Watchman, what of the night?"

India, *in her depths,* calls to the Church, *in the depths,* for it is only in the depth that the marvelous "encounter" which was willed eternally will manifest itself, in the love and in the bosom of the Father.

The grace of India is essentially a grace of call—calling to introversion. That is easily said in words, and the individual who understands it only by ear or by the intelligence has just as easily filed it away in the storehouses of his or her memory, imagining that the conceptualization of the great experience has made it fully comprehensible. In fact one who thus reduces contemplation to a conceptual given or, even more, to a life-style, is like the individual who remains on the square in front of the Temple, believing that the holy of holies has been attained.

India's secret, in a word, is that the time of parables is over (Jn. 16,25) and that never will any sign be able to satisfy the individual who really aspires to God, to the Real in itself. India goes so far in this direction that at times she forgets that man is made of flesh, that his psychism is borne by a body, that even his consciousness unveils itself only in the act, intellectual or sensory, of perception.

For the pure *advaitin*[4] in fact, there is ultimately no place neither for worship nor prayer, not even for a simple thought of adoration and of self-surrender to the Lord. To be sure, the Christian canot follow him there. He knows that he is called to participate to the very end in the ecclesial sacrament of the Body of Christ, a necessary sign for the time of the eschatological consummation of the universe. Nevertheless, how would he be able to remain indifferent to this call always farther beyond, always farther within, that the Spirit addresses to him from India?

India's true message is so secret that, actually, only a few are able to *understand* it in its very pure truth. Imitations of a speculative, emotional or even gnostic order abound and many souls allow themselves to be deceived. One dares say that only a profoundly Christian soul that has penetrated to the heart of Christ; who, like the beloved disciple has known how to listen to the heartbeats of Jesus from without and even more from within, will be able to penetrate to the deepest recesses of India's heart to gather there her most secret message for the explorer and for the Church alike.

It will surely be objected that India, even religious India, is not only the way of *Jnana,* of "wisdom" or the trans-conceptual experience of the interior mystery. And that is correct. India is immensely vast, in time and in space, and she is equally boundless in the expression of her soul. Is not Christianity itself, for that matter, of diverse character beneath its fundamental unity? India's religious proliferation in fact can be described as a tropical luxuriance. The most primitive and the loftiest forms meet together there, as also do the most concentratedly introverted and those most open to love and to service (*seva*) of the neighbor: irridiscent *lila,* [5] signs and manifestations, varying according to different temperaments and psychisms, of the mystery which man lives alone with God in the depths of his selfhood.

The tradition of India recognizes, particularly alongside

the way of *jnana*, or of the experience of wisdom, the ways of the *bhakti* or devotion and of *karma* or service.[6] There were and there still are in India admirable *bhakti*:[7] the Nayahars or the devotees of Vishna, in Tamil-Nadu; the admirable psalmist of Vithoba, Toukaram in the Maratha State; the ardent worshippers of Krishna in Bengal, to limit ourselves to three fleeting references. There were and, above all, there are now admirable "servants" (*sevak*), for example the disciples of Ghandi and Vinobha Bhave, who often shame Christians by the serious way they take Jesus' Sermon on the Mount. Even more than being parallel ways, at their summits at least, the three ways of wisdom, love and service, *jnana, bhakti, karma,* are like different expressions on the sensory and mental plane of this "passage out of the self to the depth of self" to which the Spirit has borne the soul. It is the call and the aspiration to introversion that everywhere is the center.

Is India, then, bringing to Christianity a message of introversion of which the latter, in the opinion of some, has little or no knowledge?

Actually, India brings nothing to the Christian that he or she does not already possess. Plenitude? There is no spiritual richness which is not contained in the treasure left by the Lord to his Bride. Centuries will pass and the Church will always be engaged in scrutinizing the Scriptures (Jn. 5, 39), and ceaselessly she will find in them even more marvelous riches. India comes, in its turn, at the moment chosen by God, to aid the Church, if not to discover, at least, to fructify her own treasures. Thus had God already prepared the wisdom of Egypt, of Chaldea and of Persia to illuminate the revelation made to the prophets and to the sages of Israel; later Greek wisdom set bounds to its two Testaments. The Incarnation, in fact, considered in itself and in its pleromatic conclusion, is not an event apart from the history of humanity, something applied to it as though from without, It is the fundamental event, the fulfillment to which all is conformed.

II

It is not by words that India's secret is transmittable. Words do not hold great secrets, they betray them, rather, even more than they disclose them. At best their truth can be divined behind the words. Only when the interior preparation is completed do they light up in the depths of the soul where they shine with the light proper to them.

Moreover the role of the spiritual teacher in the tradition of India is not to instruct or teach doctrines, but to communicate an experience. The true *guru* is the one who progressively leads the disciple to the point at which the spark will spontaneously fly upward in the disciple's heart; the teacher who patiently purifies the intelligence of its errors and of all that which it unconsciously superposes on the Real. Above all, he teaches the disciple how to create emptiness in the heart and mind so that the Spirit can work in full freedom.

Hinduism, in its center at least, is not a tradition of doctrines or of ritual. Rather, it is the transmission of an experience, the revelation to each one so that by oneself one can discover in it the secret that lies in the depth of each heart and which has been there from time immemorial.

The secret of God is beyond all words. All that those who came closer to touching it, regardless of the religious climate, could say of it was that it was "inaccessible."

India's secret is the call to introversion, the opening to introversion, to ever more introversion, not the teaching of anything else new—the *vedanta*[8] has nothing to teach; it is simply the awakening to what *is,* in the profoundest depth.

That is why India's secret will be transmitted in the Church only very secondarily by means of the word, writing, or university teaching. Rather, what is at issue here is more like an ontological transmission, from depth to depth, soul to soul, in the great silence.

Words and writings do not reach to the *depths* unless they

already spring up from the depths of the individual from whom they issue. They will awaken veritable echoes in souls only if they themselves are bearers of experience.

There is in fact a transmission, all too much forgotten, from soul to soul, the para-psychic phenomena of which are but a pale reflection, as far from reality as the stratosphere is from the inter-stellar spaces, which the uninformed confuse with it. When did the Apostles finally understand Jesus if not when he had disappeared from their sight, once the sound of the last of the words pronounced by him vanished? Only then could the Spirit, who had announced Jesus, come.

Any soul that penetrates within, just by doing so, deepens the Church and the Church's consciousness of herself. It thus calls the Church, as though from depth to depth, in the realization of her own mystery. Each Christian, each group of faithful, in effect, expresses and manifests in itself the *Una Catholica* as a whole, and in her, the only Lord.

That is precisely the irreplaceable role, the very *service* of the contemplatives in the Church. Unfortunately, people today understand less and less that their ministry to others can be something like this. We would like everyone to contribute by work to the construction of the City of Man; we would like people to participate somehow in the outward building of the Church (preaching, teaching etc.). All that can happen, of course, and in fact often did happen in the past. But what is essential is that everything must always come from within, as a bonus, so to speak. The changing economic conditions of society can pose new and difficult problems to contemplatives but nevertheless, for the very sake of the Church, they must maintain intact their ideal of their *diaconia,* their service, even at the risk of being misunderstood. They do not have to try to apologize for their so-called uselessness, inefficacy. Their uselessness, their silence, their solicitude, their refusal, finally, to accomplish anything whatsoever in the outer world is precisely the nature of their *service* in the

Church, the irreplaceable ministry that was entrusted to them; the testimony, perhaps increasingly indispensable, that God is beyond all and outside any sign.

The contemplative is simply there, recollected and silent, in the name of the Church in order to deepen in himself or herself the recollection and the silence of the Church, with Mary and the Apostles awaiting the Spirit *sedentes* (sitting) (Acts 2,2). The communion of saints is not an empty phrase, it is the communication of the Spirit of oneness in the mystery of the divine circumincession. Through the word the Spirit passes to the Church, passing onward from the Church through the sacraments. The Spirit also passes through directly, from depth to depth—from the depth of the Spirit, from the depth of God (cf. 1 Cor. 2,10) which is also the very depth of the soul in a state of grace, the inmost mystery of each elect, as St. Paul says (Rom. chapter 8, for example). The role of the contemplative is conjoined with the mystery of the Spirit—beyond any veil, beyond any sign. It is, in the Spirit as Spirit, performing the function of unity and of recollection, of completion and of gathering, the eschatological realization of the sacrament, the fulfillment of the "word."

India, in fact, traditionally understood the sense and the mystery of a life totally dedicated to contemplation much more than does the West. She had this intuition very early and delegated many of her sons to it at the time that Yahweh, with so much difficulty, was preparing the Hebrew people for its predestined role. The contemplative life never ceases to flower on India's soil and it is still honored there despite the degeneration of some monks and the desire for gain and social efficacy which in others now shrouds the purity of the ancient ideal. This ideal, the ideal of the *sannyasin,*[9] remains untouched, thanks be to God, with many. The *sannyasin* is free of any obligation towards human society, even towards any outward worship renderable to God. He lives alone, in the name of his brethren, alone in his mystery which is the essential mystery, simple witness to the Absolute, witness to the indescribable Presence, the libation of a people to its God, the essential and supreme ministry.

In this perspective we can now understand that it is the contemplatives who, more than anyone else, are called to this corresponding ministry in the Church of God, called to gather India's heritage for Christ, to discover in the depth of India's heart this pearl, precious above all things, which the Spirit prepares in it so they can pass it on to the heart of the Church through a kind of non-discontinuous osmosis?

To be sure there is much talk of the need for contemplative Orders in Asia and particularly in India. Unfortunately, however, this is often expressed in terms that make true contemplatives blush.

Monks and nuns are wanted for the purpose of intercession; that is all to the good, but it is only a very first step. They are also wanted for liturgical purposes, and that is better, providing that the liturgy of an essentially disinterested praise is not transformed into a means of having something else in view. At times they are also wanted in the hope that their example will impress the Hindu. Unfortunately, their presence is most often requested in connection with artisan or agricultural activities among populations whose standard of living must be raised above its wretched level.

The monastic life, necessary to India even more than elsewhere, is a life totally dedicated to the essential contemplation and is in keeping with the purest tradition of India, on the one hand, and the Christian tradition of the desert, on the other. The forms and manifestations can vary depending on the circumstances, indeed on economic necessities. But never, never, must such expressions mask the essential, neither to the eyes of the consecrated, nor to the eyes of those reached by their witness. And it goes without saying that such a monastic life must be molded materially, mentally and spiritually, in Indian life and traditions. Neither India nor the Church in India has anything in common with people who would preserve or transport a western life-style here.

Above all it is not contemplatives who are such by name or title whom the Church and India need here. Rather, both need souls truly immersed in the mystery of introversion, whatever the name or the title by which they are outwardly named.

And even less do we need contemplative institutes that are so only in name. Rather, the need is for groups of consecrated souls, of *koinonia,* according to the old word *pakhomien,* in which everything conforms to the development of a really contemplative life, and not one that is only liturgical, ascetic or pious. The aim of the Order that is authentically contemplative is to form the monk or the nun. The so-called active Orders need members to discharge the diverse activities (teaching, preaching etc.) that the Church has entrusted to them. The contemplative Orders are dedicated exclusively to the deepening of the contemplative silence in the individuals who live in them. The liturgical, intellectual, manual "activities" that can go on in them are never an aim for which it would be necessary "to recruit," as the expression goes. The idea of "contemplatives" who bestir themselves in order to find a "vocation" is simply laughable, unless one may prefer to weep upon witnessing such a lack of understanding of the real ministry of the monk. Quite to the contrary, they ought to be so content to enter and to remain in the depth—the place proper to their vocation—unconcerned about all the rest, keeping themselves available simply for the day when the Lord will finally find them ready to reveal His secrets to souls.

III

The different monastic traditions of the Church all have their place in India, each one with its proper grace, provided only that their representatives are faithful to their ideal—and in these traditions the magnificent traditions of the eastern Churches, and particularly of Russian monasticism, so close to the Indian soul, must not be forgotten.

Nevertheless it seems that the Carmelite Order is the bearer here of a grace and of a wholly special vocation.

To be sure the Carmelite Order has evolved extensively since its beginnings.

The Order loves to link itself with the prophet Elijah—the one who proclaimed: "As Yahweh lives, the God of Israel whom I serve," the one who was mysteriously led by God to Horeb and nourished miraculously along the way, and the one to whom God revealed Himself no longer in the flame of fire, as to Moses, but in the sound of a gentle breeze at the entrance to his cave, his *guha*[10] (1 Kings, 19, 12-13).

After Elijah, the Carmelite Order recognizes as its forebears all those monks and recluses who formerly peopled the deserts of the Near East, alone in their caves or their cells, consecrated to the sole ecclesial ministry of Presence. When the Carmelite Order enters history, it is under the form of *laure*[11] in which the "hermit brothers," following the Rule of the blessed Albert, live far from cities with each in his own hut, avoiding the company of the world, avoiding even the distraction of an absorbing liturgy, passing their time night and day in silence and meditation on the Law of God.

Whatever further transformations the Carmelite Order underwent when it passed to the West and, after the example of other Orders, entered many cities, does not its primitive ideal, very purely preserved by the nuns of the Second Order, always stir dreams in those in whose heart the Spirit has deposited nostalgia for great and blessed solitude?

Benedictine monks are fond of saying that they will not have to leave the stalls in which they chant the Office on the day in which they will pass from time to eternity, unlike the Jesuit or the Dominican who will have to leave their classroom desk or their academic chair.

Much more truly than Jesuits or Dominicans, Carmelites can say that their vocation is eschatological and that they will remain forever and eternally in the silence in which they are submerged here below when they reach the bosom of God and face Him by virtue of their very vocation and their ecclesial *diaconia* if, at least, one gives credence on this matter to John of the Cross. The doctor of the Carmelite Order, gathering the purest sap of the Christian mystical tradition, taught with a rare forcefulness that in the ascent towards God, ultimately, each and any sign must disappear. It is into that very silence in the bosom of God that the Church has *sent* the Carmelite.

Even more important than the praise expressed in action and in truth is the praise of the Carmelite's silence and solitude. It is eschatological in character, the great silence of the depths, of those abysses which only the Spirit of God probes (1 Cor. 2,10). The marvel lies precisely in the fact that it is not what can be chanted about God that is the loftiest, the truest but, rather, that which goes beyond all manifestation, all understanding (cf. Eph. 3,19), this beyondness beyond all that can be uttered and adored. It is only there, in truth, that God is!

Essentially, is not the vocation of the Carmelite, in the silence of prayer, to adore this incommunicability of God in the depths and, even more, to probe in the silences beyond the very contemplation of this incommunicability and of this ineffableness, in the total purity, the diaphaneity of Being?

Is there not an admirable kinship between the fundamental vocation of the Carmelite and the fundamental vocation of India? And, in truth, are not the solitaries of the Carmelite

Order more beholden than anyone else in the Church to which they belong, to immerse themselves, in the name of the Church, in the deepest mystery of India and of the Church alike? In that place where the Spirit awaits the "encounter" of the one and of the other in order to disclose the priceless pearl whose passage to the ecclesial treasure, once they are joined together, will mark the fulfillment of the destinies of India and the attainment by the Church to a new consciousness of the mystery of the Spirit?

Nevertheless the Carmelite Order, whatever its greatness and precisely because of this very greatness, must always bear in mind, like any other religious Order, indeed like the Church herself, that it is in the service of the Spirit and not vice-versa. It is not for any kind of transposition, of what is in the West that the Spirit invites the Carmelite Order to India—the Church of India already has too many of these substitutes of all kinds, and ones that weigh heavily on her. No, the Spirit invites it to bring about a new germination and a new florescence on the soil of India of this incomparable grain that the Carmelite Order is in the will of God. If the Carmelite Order hears the call it will gather a new glory; if He prefers, God will make other choices. Since it is not a prerogative of one who is not a Carmelite to comment on this matter, we shall limit ourselves to transcribing here the testimony of a soul who already for many years has been drinking deep from the purest springs that flow from the "holy mountain":

> "It is always necessary to go beyond, beyond the Carmelite Order itself, in order to find the Plenitude of which the Carmelite Order, like any contemplative Order, incidentally, desires to disclose the mystery. It is not necessary to confuse the means with the end, the cup with the marvelous liqueur that it contains . . . The soul cultivated by the Carmelite Order bears in itself the pas-

sion of silence, not just any kind of silence, however, but the weighty silence of God and of the Spirit. It preserves in itself in a vital way this attraction to the mystery in which it savors, in private and in the night, the silent gift of Being. And it is the deep sense of the 'things' of the Spirit that permit it to go beyond all means and to live fully in the depths of its 'selfhood.'

"It is not so much the Carmelite Order, but something that is beyond the Carmelite Order that must be given to India. The pure springs of the Carmelite Order must be sought in Elijah and it is this source that must in all limpidness be given to India. It is the Carmelite Order of the beginnings that must be grafted onto India, the Order of the time of the caves of Mount Carmel in its simplicity of life and its purity—without, however, rejecting the contribution with which it has been enriched while, at the same time, stripping it of all that which encumbers and weighs down on its essential thrust. And it seems that India, in her turn, would make a marvelous contribution in helping the Order to find its total flowering and to attain its Plenitude. Or, rather, India herself must conceive and engender her own Carmelite Order in the dimensions and in the measure of her aspirations and of her need of the absolute . . .

"If it is not yet the hour of realization, it is always the hour of the Spirit, and this work must be engendered in the depths and in the Invisible before all else. It is an urgent need that the roots be planted in obscurity and silence, and even in incomprehension. Nothing matters provided only that it is implanted, or better, grafted onto the soil of India and onto her soul. All that is an invisible work and one wrought in mystery and no one will ever know what was at the base of it and, even less, what was at the summit . . . But points of contact are already necessary where the Divine will come to crash on India's soil like the thunderbolt that the very least conductor can attract and force to the ground.

"All this must be lived intensely in order to do the work of the Real and in order to understand it, this *diaconia* or service of Presence in silence and in solitude. All the rest, any accomplishment whatever will never be anything else but the externalization of all that which has been engendered in the profoundest depths, like the froth overflowing the glass in which one pours champagne in torrents! For the Spirit gives himself abundantly to those who are available. As St. John insists, God does not measure out the Spirit. Let the Spirit blow, then, in violent storm, if need be, or whether it be like the lightest murmur of the breeze. For those who hearken to the Spirit in silence, the least breath suffices to spread their wings."

IV

In the spiritual literature of India there is an image that constantly recurs since the time of the Upanishads: that of the *guha*, the "cave," the "cavern of the heart." It is the hidden place, the preeminent secret place, the place nevertheless which man at all cost must discover if he wants to escape death and arrive at imperishable life.

Since the Vedic age India's thought has nostalgically attached itself to this mysterious place of the Real, the essential *domain* bearing varied names, the place of immortality and of Light, the world of Brahman and of the *devas*.[12] The Sun was considered as the symbol of this luminous world, and its already so brilliant face that it turns towards us is the sign of the sun's other face (how much more brilliant!), the one that it turns towards the eternal. The sun was the "golden gateway" that opens on the Real, the golden cup that at one and the same time contains and conceals the True, the supreme object of the soul's desire.

India's thought increasingly interiorizes itself. India soon understood that this mystery divined to be beyond "on the farthest most parts of the beyond" (Katha-Upanishad) was *within*, the inmost mystery of inwardness.

The higher one climbs, the more indefinitely do the mind-defying spaces open before it, the deeper one descends into one's own self, the deeper do the impenetrable depths likewise open all the more indefinitely. He who expends his thought in order to force himself to obtain the *beyond* can only lose himself in the attempt to extend himself in the infinity of space. But he who withdraws into himself, seeking to penetrate ever more deeply, from center to center, to his inmost self, is just as sure to founder in this space within which it is just as inaccessible.

He who seeks, seeks beyond the eye (teaches the Kena-Upanishad) and he who breathes, breathes beyond breath, and he who thinks, thinks beyond thought. Push downward into thyself as far as the "seer of the seen," "the hearer of the heard," "the thinker of the thought"—he who sees and by whom all is seen but whom no one can see, he who feels and by whom all is felt, but whom no one can feel. For how, by what means, by which organ would one be able to reach the One by whom all is seen, all is attained, all is known? He alone *is*, and he is the measure of all.

> *Who dares to say that he knows him*
> > *thereby shows clearly that he knows him not.*
> *What does he know in truth of what Brahman is,*
> > *of what he is in himself, of what he is in him, the*
> > > *thinker,*
> > *of what he is in the forces of the universe?*
> *Understood is this Brahman only by him who gives*
> > *up understanding him,*
> > *beheld in truth, only by him who no longer beholds*
> > > *him.*

Thought divines Brahman as being on the horizon of conceptual spaces. The closer it draws, the more Brahman escapes it. When, finally, it makes a spring towards him, he disappears . . .

A flash of lightning. Thou makest a sudden movement. Ah! Thy eyelid flickers. Ah! It's all over! And thou hast not been able to hold him. But in touching thee, it burned thee, and in the joy with which it filled thee, thou hast forgotten all.

Hidden in all knowledge is the intuition of the supreme mystery, like a memory—that of the flash of lightning—like that of the call to the infinite beyondness of self: the trespass of self in order to come to the depth of self, a trespass of which the physiological death is finally only a sign.

The final mystery is that this interior mystery that one uncovers in one's inmost self, in one's disappearance in one's own self, in the spaces of the heart, namely the *Atman*[13] "pure of all taint," is this very mystery that reveals himself in the most distant spaces of the beyond, the *full, immovable Brahman*[14] himself, the principle, the life and the being of All (Chandogya-Upanishad).

Whether he be over there or here, he is ungraspable, he eludes any conceptualization. He is neither here nor there, he is neither like this or like that, *neti, neti,* as the *Birhad-Aranyaka Upanishad* says. Whatever thou doest, thou canst not grasp him, whatever thou thinkest, thou canst not utter him. One can divine him only beyond the signs.

He is the Plenitude. One who attains this point has nothing else to desire. All one's doubts are resolved, all one's fetters are burst, all is transcended, birth, death, old age, joy and pain as well. One is fulfilled.

But how can one still recognize in this plenitude the little *I* that it has invaded, the little *I* that dared to penetrate it?

Plenitude here, plenitude there (sings the Isa-Upanishad)

> from that which is full springs up the full,
> from the full springs up the full;
> plenitude alone is everywhere!

Everything moves, continues the same Upanishad, in this moving world. But at the profoundest depth of this movement, in its point of origin, dwells the spirit supreme, *Isa*, the force divine.

Behind the multiple, the base of the diverse, there is the Only One, the immovable under that which moves in the world and in man alike. All run behind him, nobody ever overtakes him. All press towards him: he, without himself moving, is always there.

He is here, very near, too near for one to be able to see him. Lo, there he is, too far for one to be able to perceive him. He is within, he is the inwardness of all that which exists, and he is also the outwardness of all things. Nothing, nobody restrains him. He is free of all form, free of all composition, radiant, self-existent, immortal, non-Death itself.

The real sage is he who knows the Plenitude in the depths of self, the profoundest depth of self, in a self more inwrought than he can attain by himself, the "truest" part of the self—the Plenitude which encompasses the universe and in which the universe *is*.

It is he, this *atman,* the inner mystery, the ultimate principle of self, this brahman, the mysterious principle and the plenitude of all that which exists—with which one must not confuse any of these signs that a conceited people adores, confusing them with the Real.

He is the Light, the light of the beginnings and of the consummation as well, through which and of which all that which exists is illumined, all that which is shines brightly. He is self-luminous in the inmost spaces of the heart.

> *In the very center of the cavern of the heart*
> *He, the Only One, He, the Sole One,*
> *I supreme, as a self supreme*
> *In Himself self-luminous.*
>
> *(Sri ramana maharishi).*

He is in every element, in all he is what he is. He is in this universe, in the earth, in the heavens, in that which there is between the two. He is in the breath of man, in his senses, in his thought. In him is contained all that which moves, all that which flickers, the worlds and the inhabitants of worlds. He is greater than the greatest, smaller than the smallest, outside the grasp of thought (*Mundaka-Upanishad*).

Seek in thyself, in the depth of thyself, continues the same Upanishad: *in this cavern of the heart wherein he moves in secret, in his private domain.*

There is the mark at which thou must take aim, like the archer, without suffering thyself to be distracted.

The arrow with which to hit the mark is the *atman,* it is thyself. The bow is the wisdom of the Upanishads, it is the AUM which is its quintessence. Brahman is the mark. Aim at him and become one with the mark, like the arrow.

Forget all the rest and pass thou on to the other strand. Here alone is the bridge towards the other shore of death.

Behold, everywhere there is nothing but Brahman: Brahman who alone is resplendent everywhere. Brahman above, Brahman below, Brahman in front, Brahman behind, Brahman to the right, Brahman to the left; Brahman alone who everywhere is infinitely effulgent.

In truth, of this Brahman nothing can be said save that he *is, asti (Katha-Upanishad),* the Yahweh of the mountain of Horeb (Ex. 3, 14).

Only *he* is. Nothing was, nothing will ever be save him!

The last rigging required in order to attain this Brahman (*Katha-Upanishad*), the skiff in which to make the crossing over to the other bank of the heart's space (*Maitri-Upanishad*) is the meditation on the *pranava*,[15] the mysterious syllable AUM (or OM)—that which alone remains in the mind when all has moved on and in the mystery of which is effected the "passage" to the Real, that which vanishes and blossoms in this very "passage."

Man begins by positioning himself facing God, by beholding Him in the reflection and in the image of the creatures, in the reflection of the saints and their experiences, in the reflection of the Scriptures that give the loftiest revelation of Him that man is capable of understanding. Borne on these magnificent states of an all-embracing contemplation, little by little, he enters into the mystery of his heart, into the abysses of self, into this image of God which he is at the profoundest depths of his own self. He first imagines God to himself, then he thinks God and purifies his heart in thinking of Him. But the more he descends into his own self, the more he realizes that this God whom he adores is beyond any thought, that He is more beautiful, greater than any conceived beauty or grandeur, that no peace, no felt joy are the peace that is essential to the beholder and which alone can satisfy the one who seeks Him. Man then loses his foothold, his thought suffocates like a castaway engulfed by a wave and whose lungs vainly try to breathe in the life-sustaining air.

Everything has disappeared from the horizon of the soul, from his thought, from his consciousness, everything on which he supported himself until then, in the worlds below as well as in the worlds above, in the world of signs, including the sublimest among them. It is the impenetrable night, the one that separates the waning of the moon from the break of dawn. It is an intolerable agony and tension for the individual who refuses to disappear and who struggles against the Being that he or she is in the depths of self. It is an agony, however, that draws to a close in an untroubled and deep slumber when the soul finally succumbs and lets itself be gathered inwardly more and more and lets itself be led further into the great silence of Being. At first it is a solitude that is felt as something frightful, a solitude of frustration, of exclusion. Finally it becomes a solitude of fullness and infinite gratification.

All the words have vanished. One after the other, words and concepts have faded on praying lips, in the thought and in the heart of the individual who was engaged in the combined contemplation and worship. All that remains in the mind—the last state—is the AUM of the ancient Vedic tradition: the primordial vowel, the *a* subdued in *o* (au) and prolonged in the nasal resonance that is *m*, a resonance that soon itself is lost in the great silence of the beginnings. The AUM has four parts, says the *Mandukya-Upanishad:* the three letters that compose it and which together yield a unique and indissociable sound and, finally, the "fourth," that which is beyond all audible sound . . .

When the consciousness, beyond all, has finally attained this greater silence, there is then plenitude, beatitude, truth, immortality, there is a vision of Being. The golden gate has swung open at one bound, the golden cup that contained the Real, has been raised. Man arrives at the very bosom of the mystery where he had sought himself, where he had sought his God. He has sought and now in this discovery he escapes from himself in the infinite resplendence of Being in the infinite Plenitude and Oneness of Being. There is only The-One-Who-Is, always and evermore ineffably alone with no other apart from Him, no matter who, *ekam eva-advityam*[16] (*Chandogya-Upanishad*).

Philosophers will come and will try to understand and to translate the ineffable experience into formulas. The individual who was thus immersed in his inmost self is speechless; he does not know how to say anything, neither of his own self, nor of God, nor of the world. His experience is solely that he has probed the infinite mystery, suffused in it, all he can do is murmur: AUM, *a-dvaita* not-two, not other. Within and without, him, thou, me, have vanished, all that which is has vanished. Immersion in the Plenitude of Being.

> *Beyond the self*
> *outside any limit to me,*
> *in the plenitude of self,*
> *at last self!*

The devout person is both astonished and scandalized that thereafter the *jnani* no longer adores. But how could he continue his adoration: who, after all, remains to be adored? In order to adore does not one have to adopt a position apart and face the object of adoration? Is the infant at his mother's breast able to look at her and to distinguish between itself and her? It is a mysterious return to the most primordial sources.

It is this precisely, this intuition that springs up in the heart of those whom the Self has *chosen (Katha-Upanishad),* this implacable experience of Presence who, for centuries and millennia, attracted so many of India's children into the most a-cosmic vocation imaginable: wandering along roads, from village to village, paying no attention whatsoever to the things of this earth, hardly uttering a word except at times in order to recall to those whom they meet the secret of the profoundest depth and, at noon, begging a handful of rice from the houses they happened to be passing by—or hidden in the forest solitudes or in mountain caves, their gaze fixed on inwardness, witnesses of Being.

And if it was not this most ineffable of experiences which thus hurled them out of the world and made it impossible for them to work further in the City of Man, it was, at least, due to their gurus or the Scriptures whose secret had pierced their soul, stripping them of any taste for all that which is mere appearance—a dawn still barely discernible, perhaps, but which already in the depth of the heart presages and prepares the high noon of realization.

At the end of the last century, in Medurai, Tamil-Nady, there lived a youngster who studied grammar and the sciences at the local high school. He was a lad bursting with health, sportive and ready to fight at the drop of a hat. One morning as he was seated in his home, the idea suddenly struck him that he was doomed to die. At first his entire being trembled at the thought. Soon, however, the young brahman regained his self-control: "I die? So be it!", and, stretching himself out on the floor, he acted out in all lucidity the drama of death. He felt life as though it were retracting in him: the warmth receded from his members, his thought took wing, his consciousness seemingly evanesced. Everything that was *him* was on the point of disappearing—when, suddenly, the light dawned: everything passes away, everything goes away, *me,* I remain, *I am*! At a bound the youth had penetrated to the last secrets of the heart, he had attained to the last abyss of Being, to the deepest center of the *guha*, the cave, to the other shore of self, the shore of the naked and total truth of *self.*

Several days later his parents at home and his teachers at the school launched a futile search for the boy. The parents did not learn of his whereabouts until several years later: he was seated on the sacred mountain of Arunachala, silent, naked and alone in one or the other of the hollows in the rocks, fixed on Self.

Crowds of people, from India and beyond, hastened to see the *darshana*—to behold the face of Ramana Maharisi, the face that reflected the transparence of Being and of the unique experience. Ramana, however, was only a sign and a symbol: the sign of all those in whom the Self manifests itself "alone and with no other" but which remains unknown to men, guarded, so to speak, in the secret gardens of the Lord. He was also the call to all people that at the profoundest depths of their own selves, the Spirit also awaits them.

In India there will always be the likes of Ramana, the sage

of the caves of Arunachala, of Sadisiva, the naked, silent wanderer of Kavery,of Ramalinga, who "passed" in an aura of light.

May God soon provide the visible Church of India with worthy imitators of these people!

V

The echoes of such experiences that spring up in the Hindu soul and that are expressed in the Scriptures, or in the chants of saints, were bound to evoke extraordinary resonances in the depths of the Christian soul—in that, at least, which beyond external practices and theological speculations, and conducted by the Spirit of wisdom, has penetrated to the mystery of the heart of Jesus, to the profoundest depth of its own self.

The Christian also knows that God is "beyond." He knows that God is free of all space, within as well as without. He knows that there is truly nothing else that exists outside God, that all comes from Him, that all goes to Him, that in Him is all that which there is, that in Him lives all that which lives, that He is the light with which every consciousness is illumined (Jn. 1), that, nevertheless, this Light is inaccessible (1 Tim. 6) and that nobody has ever beheld God (Jn. 1, 18). He knows, further, that no concept of theology will ever succeed in giving sufficient expression to the experience that the saints had of their life in the Spirit, even less to the consciousness that Jesus has of being of the Father and of whom he made us part.

The Spirit himself, in truth, is in the depths—the bottommost depths—of those who were called and who received from Jesus the power to become children of God. It is the Spirit who moves them from within, like a principle of their acts, closer to their own selves than any consciousness that they can have of their own selves—this same Spirit who proceeds from the Father and from the Son in an ineffable mystery of oneness, of *advaita,* the Spirit who rested on Jesus, in whom Jesus offered himself at death and rose from the dead, the Spirit whom Jesus unreservedly communicates to his disciples in the name of the Father. It is the Spirit who, from the non-duality or oneness of Being eternally realized in the Plenitude of the Three, cries out in us the call to Plenitude and murmurs the essential word: *Abba*, Father. For, as St. Paul says (1 Cor. 6,17) " . . . anyone who is joined in the Lord is one spirit with him."

The Spirit so possesses the Christian that Paul, from his own personal experience, can say in all truth, but in formulas which make the words explode, that there is no longer either Greek, or Jew, neither slave nor freedman—hence neither *this one* or *that one*—but only Jesus, the Son, eternally and in time opposite the Father, *omnia in omnibus,* (Eph. 1, 23).

Jesus, in effect, communicated to us all of his own self and, therefore, as such, all of the Spirit, all of the Father. His last confidences before he delivered himself for our salvation can leave no room for doubt on this score (Jn. 17):

"Father, may they be one in us, as you are in me and I am in you."

"With me in them and you in me, may they be so completely one that the world will realize that it was you who sent me and that I have loved them as much as you loved me"—with this Love that is the Spirit, in this Oneness that is the Spirit.

Elsewhere He had said:

"I know my own and my own know me, just as the Father knows me and I know the Father" (Jn. 10, 14-15).

"As I, who am sent by the living Father, myself draw life from the Father, so whoever eats me will draw life from me. This is the bread come down from heaven; not like the bread our ancestors ate; they are dead, but anyone who eats this bread will live forever" (Jn. 6, 57-58).

On the last evening of his mortal life, Jesus announced to his disciples his departure and his return, at one and the same time.

"In a short time the world will no longer see me" (Jn. 14, 19); "But I shall see you again" (Jn. 16,22). And this will transpire in the Spirit whom he promises at the same time—in the oneness, in the *advaita* of the Spirit, in a consciousness so intimate by connaturality, says St. Thomas, that thought cannot even conceive it.

In the Upanishads or in India's mystical tradition there is in reality no sense or no dimension of interiority, no revelation of oneness or non-quality that is not found in the Christian revelation. The Christian whom the Upanishads might frighten should be rather afraid to open the gospel of St. John or to read the letters of St. Paul. And these Christian scriptural texts are all the more remarkable because they are inscribed in a cultural and religious context deeply marked by the grandiose vision of the prophets of Israel who, on the horizon of their thought and also on that of history and of the cosmos, had seen rise up before them, Yahweh, the preeminent Other.

India's mystical tradition contributes nothing in itself to the Christian which the latter does not already know. Nevertheless it is an infinitely precious grace of God bequeathed to His Church so that she might deepen the revealed mystery, that of the Spirit above all, of the correlative intimacy of the Father and of the Son, the mystery of the Oneness of the Plenitude, of the Pleroma. To be sure the formulations of the Upanishads will strike anyone who was raised in other spiritual climes as abrupt and paradoxical: but it is precisely in that way that they jolt the mind and do not allow it indolently to rest in the world of signs and of concepts in which it delights. Above all it is not the words that are of prime importance here, but rather the message which these words, tirelessly but always inadequately, try to convey. One who listens to the Upanishad in that part of the heart from which it springs, from the depth of the soul of the *rishis,* will hear at every new reading an ever more abyssal echo and resonance. Each time one will believe that he has discovered everything, and each time one finds oneself still learning matters beyond any knowledge.

They are not words that must be gathered and investigated. They are rather a call that plumbs the depths, that *aspires* to descend to the depths. It is this wind of the abysses that carries away and engulfs one, the wind that on the day of Pentecost filled and shook the place where the Apostles had gathered for the Cenacle, a figure of the Church.

Does it not suffice for the Christian to meditate on the notion that God is in him or her, whereupon one is swept up in the whirlwind discussed earlier in connection with the meditation of the Hindu?

God is in me—as Theresa of Avila had discovered long before the theologians taught it to her. He is there as cause, say these same theologians, through the immensity of His presence; He is also there through grace, in the communication of the inward trinitarian life.

He is there, and I try to picture this presence to myself. I begin by imagining it, by localizing it, so to speak, within me, in some "place" of my body or of my soul. Like Peter on Tabor, I dream of building there a tabernacle where I would come to withdraw within myself and worship as I do in the churches.

Unfortunately, I soon feel that all my efforts are in vain. How to enclose in a temple, in a tabernacle, the one whose Presence causes all places to shatter? There is no place in me nor any place else in which He is not already ensconced long before I even thought of establishing him there. It is like a light, a fire, that has already invaded all, illumined all, consumed all, even before the spark that purposed to kindle it, ignited. There is no space that is not his, that does not vibrate with his Presence, neither in my body nor in my soul, nor in my thought, nor in my consciousness, nor in the most secret spaces of my heart.

He who enters into his own self in order to behold God, to pray to him, to worship him, to prostrate himself before him, to cry out his call to be invaded by him, illumined by him, possessed by his Spirit—no matter where he tries to position himself opposite him, he finds that the place is already taken, that the fire has consumed all, that the wind has filled all, that the Spirit has invaded all.

I try to think at the profoundest depth of my consciousness, I try to reach the bottom-most recess of my being. There—where I am *me*, this point, this essence of my soul in which I, so and so, incommunicably, irreplaceably *am*, this depth of myself that dominates all, that is not swept away in the current of universal evolution, this "place" of mine where from my teachers I have learned that I participate ineffably in God, in which I respond personally to the call that God addresses to me from the depth of his eternity.

The lower I descend, the more I immerse myself in my profoundest depth, in my truest self, in the hope of worshipping more veritably there, of crying out *my Abba, Father* there—all the more inexorably, more implacably annihilating is this Presence who leaves nothing to subsist, who unremittingly wrests from the soul all the signs under which it had lived until then.

" . . . My mirror darkens before its conflagration. No name subsists in its memory (not even mine) which could be cried out to Him . . . Nothing more save the confession of His sacred solitude . . . diaphanous shroud of the between us two, impalpable feminine veil of silence . . . " (L. Massignon, *Parole donnée,* p. 252).

Even before I was able to pronounce the I which would refer me to Him, or better to the Thou which, at least, preserves in the privacy of his reciprocity the I that cries out, this Thou—the unique and eternal *I* has already reverberated in the abysses of my heart and invaded all therein, resounding with such an amplitude that nothing else in it can make itself heard.

> the *I AM, ehieh asher ehieb, of Horeb*
> the *I AM, aham asmi[17] of the Upanishads*
> the *triple aham of the Plenitude of Being, that*
> *Jesus revealed to us.*

He is in the depth of my being. No, not Him. Nor even any longer Thou. Thou presupposes me, Thou presupposes I. And who subsists apart in order to speak of Him? I, I, *aham, aham,* the unique and absolute I, the I of the Unique One—the depth of my depth in which alone *I* can express myself; but then I no longer know how to express myself save in the total plenitude of Being.[18]

There are two processions in God: that through the method of beholding and that through the method of love; that through the method of speech and as though an expansion of self, that through the method of recollectedness and self-reflection, that method which is disclosed in the presence of the One to the other, of God and of his Son, that method which is disclosed in the eternal non-duality of the Father and of the Son.

There is no face to face experience that is not fulfilled in the beatifying experience of Oneness—for the Son is not until he attains completion in the Plenitude of the Spirit, the consummation of God in the deepest recesses of the bosom of God.

And there is no experience of oneness that does not end up in the *face to face* from which it springs.

That is a mystery of faith, and man knows of it only in the revelation of it made to him by the One who eternally remains in the bosom of the Father; and there is no true experience of the encountered presence of God save in the consciousness of it had by Jesus, Son, creature, substitute of man the sinner.

The experience of non-duality that Indian Scriptures transmit to us is no doubt the highest summit attainable by man, even guided by the Spirit, as long as God had not yet revealed Himself in His Son; for the Spirit was as though fettered as long as Jesus had not yet risen from the dead (cf. Jn. 7, 39) and the Word had not yet disclosed its full mystery.

At the time when the *rishis* of India were undergoing their blissful experience of the non-duality of Being in the Mind, the prophets of Israel were also fascinated by the Presence that hung over them and just as implacably placed opposite to them; and by this voice, the *Dabar* Yahweh, which did not allow them even the possibility not to talk so that they could proclaim the One who was to come, so that they could cry out to the people about their sins.

The prophets of Yahweh were the heralds of the Word; the *rishis* of India, the privileged witnesses of the Silence of God.

Had they met, probably neither Elijah the Prophet nor Yasnavalkya, the *Rishi*, would have recognized or understood each other for, humanly speaking, they were approaching each other from totally opposite slopes of the holy Mountain. Nevertheless both of them were precursors of Christ.

All would culminate in Christ alone: the Word and the Silence of God. He was the Word of God issued from the silence of the Father (St. Ignatius of Antioch) and from him proceeds the Spirit to whom no name can be given. In him were concluded, at one and the same time, the preparations of the prophetic religions, of which Israel was the privileged type, and of the so-called mystical religions that were developing over in the distant East. If the prophetic *face to face* with God obtained in the consciousness of Jesus a reality that no prophet could have divined, in the depth of his heart there also opened a *guha* that no Upanishad would have ever been able to penetrate—for in the depth of the heart of Christ there is the bosom of the Father.

It was in the Revelation of the Word, in the religion of the prophets, that God was to proclaim himself. The man whom he had made was flesh and thought. Hence He had chosen a people and prophets in order to prepare the coming in the flesh of His Son, the Word, *Dabar* Yahweh.

But the experience of the Word must be consummated in Silence, a silence of expansion and of communion in a moment of final recollectedness, an experience of being a Beholder of the experience of divine non-duality. And it is with this in view that God prepared India from Vedic times, and with it the whole world of the Far East which, through Buddhism, lives from India's original spiritual intuition.

Again, however, it was not a complement of Divine Revelation that the Spirit prepared for the Church in India. The election of Israel remains unique, and also unique in His plan is the Mediterranean air of culture in which the Church spent, almost entirely, her first millennia—the Noachic world of the Bible—and in which the Church was constituted intellectually and institutionally. This was necessary to the Church since man is mind, since he is community. What the Church needed was a deepening consciousness difficult to express—something so mysterious, something as unsignifiable as the second trinitary procession which leaves theology mute. For if the spirit springs up from the Word and is witness of the Word, it defies all word. It is this final resonance of AUM in which all is silent. If the Spirit reveals the Word, as Jesus promised, it is in the same depths from which the Word springs up in the bosom of the Father.

If the passage of the *advaitin* experience to the trinitarian experience of the Christian faith is, like all passages to God, death and resurrection and, therefore, involves a profound participation in the dark night of the holy Agony, so does the passage of the Christian through the dark night of the Vedantic experience bring with it a grace of intense purification. St. John of the Cross, more than anyone else, has analyzed the illusions indulged in by the spiritual, conceptual and subliminal elements which the mind superposes on real experience, thus demonstrating the necessity of an inexorable purification in the one whom God calls. The encounter with the Vedantic experience is a veritable dark night of the soul for the Christian, and in him, for the whole Church. It encompasses all the human states of the self-existent, supportless Presence, thus making man realize that his being is pure gift, pure effusion of love, that he is nothing or rather that he is only of God, that he cannot be anything else but of God, *vivit Deo* (Rom. 6,10), who makes him experience in the profoundest depths of his own self the experience of death, the sole bearer of the grace of the resurrection.

In the depth of the experience of non-duality there is only the undivided plenitude of Being, the *I,* eternal, unique and absolute. In the paschal dawn, which is that of the experience of faith, it is as though this *I* resounded trebly in its own self, as though this plenitude spread and trebly communed with itself. Nevertheless for the soul that awakens from the great slumber in this dawn and to this audition, it is not as though it hears it from outside itself—for the soul, in that liberating night, was healed forever more from imagining or from conceiving anything whatsoever outside God. It is within this very *aham,* one and eternal, that the soul awakens and recovers itself. It is in the Thou that the Father eternally utters to the Son that the soul re-finds itself in Presence, in the unique *face to face,* as Scripture makes clear to those who know how to understand it:

> *"Thou art my Son, the Lord's word came to me, I have begotten thee this day"* (Ps. 2—Introit of Christmas Day, first Mass at midnight).

"I have risen and am still with thee" (Ps. 138, Introit of Easter Sunday).

"Now I can lie down and go to sleep and then awake, for Yahweh has hold of me" (Ps. 3).

It is in this very presence of the Son to the Father, in this non-dual depth of the One and the Other, in which their reciprocal gaze wells up, that the soul finally recovers itself individually, in the incommunicability that is proper to it, in the irreplaceableness of its vocation, of its pre-destination, of the "doxology" that it is—that the soul hears pronounced its new name, its true name, of which the one given to her by humans or that which it tried to discover in the depth of its consciousness are nothing else but pale reflections. Now it is in total truth that in this Presence the soul can indeed cry: *Abba,* my Father; *Eloi,* my God.

This is not the place to deepen the experience of Christian faith, above all that experience, so pure and so radiant, that springs up beyond the *advaitine* night that it is.[19] Known as it is by God alone and to the one in whom it discloses itself, even less than the experience of non-duality, no words can give an account of it. It suffices to have pointed to the path. He who knows has understood: *qui habet audiendi.*

It is to the discovery of the pearl in the depths of one's own heart that India has led the Christian. In the footsteps of the *rishis,* beyond the *rishis,* India invites him or her to penetrate to the mystery of oneness from which, as though anew, the soul of the glorious and effulgent Presence will rise on the soul's horizon. And this presence will never more disappear as in the case of the *rishis* because the Christian is the very One who in eternity beholds the face of the Father, and because in the depth of the Christian's spirit there is the Spirit who probes in it the depths of God, in faith.

India calls the Christian, India calls the Church to this experience of the depths of God.

And the Spirit calls the Christian to it, and the Spirit calls the Church to it, the Spirit who through all the events of time and all that which humankind does, reminds humankind of what Jesus said.

And through India the Spirit also re-tells the Church and the consecrated souls of the holy Church that the annihilating experience of the absolute leads directly to the *sannyasa,* thereby recalling to Christian nuns and monks the adamantine purity of their vocation.

May the Carmelite Order hearken to this voice for it should be sensitized to it more than anyone else in the Church.

It is for the Epiphany, for the *Parousia* of the Lord that the Spirit calls the Church in India. *Donec veniat*!

For the revelation of the Lord in the profoundest depth of the silence of the Spirit—for the opening to the *face to face*—for the breaking of the dawn in which, on the uncircumscribed Ocean of the non-duality and of the silence of Being, the Father eternally begets the Son.

"Come," say the Spirit and the Bride together, "Let everyone who listens answer, 'come,' " (Rev. 22,17).

For the *Parousia* of the Lord takes place in the soul's depths. The Church of India will not truly be founded until in the depths of a soul, which has fallen asleep in the Spirit of the great *advaitine* slumber of the *rishis,* finally arises the Risen Christ, crying *Abba, Pater.*

Veni Domine.

Chapter 5

The Priest for Whom India Waits,

for Whom the World Waits!

India awaits him, the world awaits him.

Indeed, at times, this priest is already in India as well as in the world. His presence is rarely blazoned forth, however, save when God wills to stir up the Church. Most often he is hidden, ignored save by some, by those in whom the Spirit has taken up its abode and who, as though by instinct, led by this same spirit, go to him. Such is the priest for whom India hearkens, for whom the world *hearkens.*

Thus Pope John was this quite simple priest for whom the world had been waiting, for whom the world had been hearkening.

I

The Christian priest, in the context of India, can be only a guru. And here indeed it seems that the Spirit has something to say to the Church through India.

For the Hindu, the guru is not just simply any preacher who simply repeats to one willing to listen what he has learned from teachers or read in their manuals. He is a man who speaks from experience. The guru is the one who dispenses the teaching of salvation: is it not only from the depth of the heart that one knows the mystery of wisdom, that the experience of salvation springs up?

The guru or spiritual teacher can be only an individual who

one day found in the depth of his soul the "true and living" God, of whom the Bible speaks on every page, and who from that moment onwards and throughout the rest of his life is marked by the scorch of this encounter just as Jacob was permanently lamed in consequence of the encounter at the ford of Jabbok, just as the skin on the face of Moses shone so much when he came down from the mountain of Sinai.

The guru is the one who, having discovered in the depth of his heart the spark of Being—not an abstraction but the I AM who manifested himself on Horeb—henceforth can no longer fail to recognize it everywhere within and without each creature, each human being, in the inmost core of all that which exists, of each event, or each movement of the cosmos that measures time.

In his quest for the Real, of course, he was helped by books—above all the books that his tradition has bequeathed to him and which communicate to him, to the extent that communication is possible, the experience of those pioneers who have access to the inner mystery.

No doubt they also must have been helped by the teachers, for it is only from *others* that the salvation teaching is received, as the Upanishad (Karma 2, 7-9) attests. This is what Paul, for his part, recalled to the Romans (10, 14-15). This teaching in fact is not only communication, it is also communion as one would say in Christian terminology. But the great secret lies precisely here. The role of the Teacher is not to transmit *notions*. His role, above all else, is to awaken the disciple. His role is to open the inner eye, the eye that immerses itself in interiority and in that perspective recognizes mystery.

Further, his role is to open the mind of the disciple to the Spirit who dwells in him, to that Spirit who probes and scrutinizes the depths of God.

The words pronounced by the guru, of course, pass from the mouth to the ear externally, as does all human speech that necessarily spreads itself through the ambient air. But, in an even more true manner, the word of the guru is transmitted directly from heart to heart through this unifying medium who is the Spirit, the communion of all in the eternal Word.

And this is why in India silence is considered a privileged medium for the teaching of wisdom.

The Word proceeds from Silence as Ignatius, the great bishop of Antioch, taught. And it is only in the silence of the Spirit that the Voice can be heard. Only the Spirit can make the Word be understood, as Jesus affirmed. When the Voice became silent on the earth, the Spirit appeared in tongues of fire on the heads and in the hearts of the disciples. The knowledge of the mystery of God is transmitted only by means beyond words.

II

Christianity too often was reduced by men to its social, institutional, ritual, intellectual forms. And the ecclesial *diaconia* or service appeared too often also as a simple exterior ministry.

Whereas Christianity, before all else, is experience: the experience that Jesus the son of Mary, Jesus the Galilean, the Word consubstantial with the Father, had of God his Father. The experience of the Father in the Christ and in the Spirit.

It is from the experience of the Father in the depth of the soul of Jesus that the Church sprang up in the dimension of time. The Father is known only when the Spirit is given in all plenitude. Jesus came to this earth precisely in order to be the bearer of this plenitude of Spirit, Life.

Christianity is Life, the very life of God in the bosom of the Blessed Trinity communicated to man through grace.

Jesus came down to earth in order to give us life, so that men might possess life and possess it evermore with greater abundance. The Spirit that he communicates to us is a new

Elan in effect, it is the gushing forth from the infinite Source who is the Father.

Life, of course, is already found in our body, in this particle of animated matter in which we awaken to being. And it is in the body of Christ, as St. Paul teaches, that all is conjoined in being, and hence also in our body. Nevertheless the life that manifests itself in this body is but an expression, shifting and transient, of a life that lies more deeply within. The body fades and wanes but constantly renews itself. Finally there comes the day when it is no longer even able to be this sign and it is re-absorbed in the current of cosmic evolution.

Life, undoubtedly, is also in intelligence, in thought, the concept of the word. And it is not in thought nor in word, if not in The One who is the Word, the Logos of the Father. Thought itself, however, is only sign. It fades and transforms itself; it disappears in slumber. Not even its "forms" can survive death.

The experience of God cannot depend on whether man is physically asleep or awake, nor on circumstances that may have permitted him to furnish his mind with more or less sublime concepts.

The awakening of man to God transpires on a level of the soul much deeper than any level attained by thought—the place that the Upanishads call the *guha,* the cave of inwardness, the inmost crypt.

Life, as a matter of fact, is only there. All the rest, the body, the senses, the mental word as uttered is never anything else but sign, a sign that passes away.

Life is there, for it is there that the eternal mystery of man springs up in the depth of each individual consciousness. It is there that the Father calls each one in his Son, the Holy One. It is there that each one hears this call and responds to it freely in the Spirit.

The Christian experience is just that. To convince oneself of this it suffices to re-read St. John and to become attentive to the words that he heard from Jesus when he leaned against his breast on the evening of Holy Thursday. The Christian experience is the trinitarian experience, the experience of Jesus himself in which, through him, all are called to participate.

III

It is to this awakening in God in the depth of souls to which the Church is conformed, with all her sacraments, all her ministries.

All the rest is just sign, preparations of a more or less related character. As soon as the priest forgets the essential purpose of his *diaconia,* the *res,* he reduces his ministry to a technique of a human order and the Church to a simple phenomenon of a sociological order.

If Christianity, notwithstanding, endures and progresses, it is because the Spirit, despite all, ever blows in the depths of souls and continues to realize the *res* of the sacrament, of the plenary sacrament which the Church is before all else.

God, however, willed to avail himself of men. And more than anyone else the priest is in the service of God. He is the one on whom first of all falls the obligation to awaken souls to God in the profoundest depth of their own selves.

The priest is the minister of the Word. He is the one who, in virtue of his office, repeats among men the word pronounced by God when He created, when He aroused the prophets, when He incarnated Himself. He is, above all, the minister of the Word that ransomed us, when Christ offered himself to the Father for the sake of humankind in celebrating the holy Supper. All the words of the priest, all his thoughts, all his life, converge toward this consecratory Word which he repeats every day. They converge toward it but, even more, they all issue from it as though from a sacred Source which, through the word and the life of the priest, spreads everywhere in the world.

The solitary in the Church is the minister of the Silence of God, The priest is the voice of the Voice. Just as the Church *sends* the hermit to the desert, likewise does she *send* the priest in the very thick of the world, in the very thick of humanity like a sacramental grain in the very midst of creation so that through his word may arise the eschatological mystery with which creation is pregnant since the very beginning.

The priest also pronounces the eucharistic word through which the definite Day of the final resurrection is made present in each instant of Time, and the mystical word which, springing up from the depths, penetrates to the profoundest depth of souls that hear it and reveals in them the Spirit.

The priest speaks, teaches, absolves, consecrates, and all that in the name of Christ. At times he makes a human glory of it, alas! More often, however, he is just too exhausted to bear such a responsibility.

As a matter of fact it is no small thing to be an instrument of God. Man cannot be an inert instrument. God made him free, all is given to him, all in man is something *received:* nevertheless nothing is given to him save in the very act through which he freely accepts it. In the continued work of creation as in that of redemption, man is the free cooperator of God—this *synergy* of which the theology of the East speaks so magnificently.

To be sure the priest is not the Instrument of a distant Christ, of a Christ whose earthly existence would be confined to times past and whose present-day existence would be spent in a heaven different from our world. No, the Heart of Christ beats in the very depth of the heart of the priest. The priest is the minister and the privileged instrument of the Son present at the very source of his being.

The priest is before all else the one who transmits the experience that Jesus, as man, made of God his Father.

It was to reveal the Father that the Son of God became

man. To reveal Him through his words and through his deeds alike: through his love for humankind which manifested the infinite and eternal Love of the Father, through his obedience to the Father which led him to the Cross, through his Resurrection which placed him opposite the Father in the very flesh of his humanhood, and through his Ascension, which finally proclaimed and initiated the final return of all to the Father.

Thus the Son of Man willed, so to speak, to undergo his own unique experience of eternal awakening to the Father as man and in time. For it was at the time of his very experience as man that the words and deeds would naturally spring up and which would directly reveal to men the mystery of their Heavenly Father and thus lead them to the profoundest depth of his Heart.

The Church is the continuation in the Spirit of this experience of Jesus. She is the front line of the world that comes back to God in the Spirit, *transiturus*. . . . The Church is the witness in the world of her own beginnings, which the world has forgotten. The Church is the divine call to each human being, to this depth deeper than self, which human beings overly tend to forget. The Church is the reminder that deeper than all joy, than all peace, is the beatitude and essential serenity of Being; that even deeper than this existential anxiety that marks our time, there is the cry of Jesus in Gethsemani and on Calvary. It is this cry of Jesus in each human being addressed to the Father that the Church, and first of all the priest, is charged to recall.

IV

The baptismal character and the priestly character reach a truth in the profoundest depth of being. They effect an ontological transformation in it. It is at the inmost center of his personal life that baptism places man opposite God and that ordination assigns the priest the mission of awakening each one to this *face to face*.

The person who is Christian only at the level of notions and concepts or, even more, only on the level of external rites, is unfaithful to his call and because of his negligence he remains infinitely this side of what he is in reality.

And even more unfaithful is the priest who contents himself with the mere performance of rites, with preaching repetitiously and by rote, and with seeking his own selfish purposes in this world in the name of God and the Church, the priest in whom the ministry and the apostolate do not flow from an inmost Source which in him is the Spirit bringing all back to the Father.

It is the salt that has lost its savor and good only to be trodden underfoot. It is the nourishment that is neither hot nor cold and that gives the Lord nausea.

One can transmit only what one has oneself. No one can awaken a sleeper if one is asleep oneself. No one can awaken another to the beatific light of the divine experience if in the depth of one's own soul one's own eyes are not opened to God.

Let us be properly understood. It is not a question here of para-mystical or para-psychical phenomena. It is in the faith that all transpires, as St. John of the Cross admirably expounds it. The sign of this awakening is not found in the sublimity of notions that by chance are born in the Intellect, even less in the feelings of fervor and the ardent desires that, at times, makes the soul deeply feel that it is acting for God. Before all else this awakening is manifested in a profound attitude of the soul that gives a special savor to all that which it hears, meditates and utters of God, a certain very particular touch to all that it does for its brethren in the name of God, and finally in an indefinable something which shows that it has gone beyond all selfishness, all hope of personal reward, that it has attained to the depth of self, to the very source of self, to the Spirit that now is in the soul as the only principle of all that the soul is and of all that the soul does—"the Spirit who himself *moves* those who are the children of God."

When this type of priest, awakened within himself and moved by the Spirit, is largely scattered throughout the Catholic world, there is no doubt that then people will again become totally attentive to the message that the priest is charged to transmit, there is no doubt that the world will again start to hearken to the Church.

For the Spirit is also there, here in India, everywhere in the world, the Spirit who, beyond all forces, dwells in the depth of each human heart, the Spirit who calls and the Spirit who waits—the Spirit who, *while waiting,* cannot abandon souls but lets them develop each according to its own possibilities until Christians, and first of all their priests, finally offer the message of the Lord at the level of interiority where the Spirit waits.

V

All is conformed to this Encounter in the depth of hearts, an encounter of the soul and God, the manifestation to the world of the creation of the eternal *face to face* of the Son and of the Father in the oneness of the Spirit; conformed to this return to the Father towards which Jesus sighed and to which he has invited us all.

Here is the encounter and return to that toward which all in the history of the world and in the unfolding of the redemptive mystery is working. It is an encounter and return in the heart of each human being with a view to that which God has willed or permitted in each one of the circumstances and happenings that encompass and lead each human life.

It is an encounter and return in which time draws to a close in eternity: the *Fiat Lux* (Let there be light) that springs up from the very Source in every human consciousness that awakens to God.

The priest is the pre-eminent minister of this Encounter in the Church and in the world.

The Spirit awaits, in the depth of hearts, for the contact to be made from which the light will spring up—the contact with the heart of a true priest in which the Spirit is free and from which he has expelled all darkness.

Techniques, of course, are necessary to a priest in his apostolate. He does not have the right to make light of any of the gifts of God, nor of any of those instruments which God gives to man through the countless inventions and discoveries of our time. Nor does he have the right to scorn learning and it is his bounden duty to study the sacred texts of Scripture and of Tradition with all possible care.

The priest must make use of all that. But he must make use of it for God alone. Otherwise the means would become an end and he would be renewing Lucifer's transgression. All is in his service, but he is in the service of the only Lord.

He was not ordained priest of Christ simply in order to repeat a text or gestures learned in advance like actors on a stage or speakers over the radio.

He is in the service of an experience, that of the Lord Jesus, an experience which had been communicated to him just so that he in turn may communicate it to souls. It is this experience in him which is the source of his whole priestly life, which gives value and apostolic efficacy to everything he says and does as priest. It is this experience which in him, as in St. Paul, leaves him no other possibility save that of dedicating himself with his whole heart to an extension of the kingdom of God.

It can happen that his word is withheld or appears unutterable. Its message will pass nevertheless from the Source through him, for it can never be obstructed. There are in fact places and also times in history—even in the history of each individual—in which silence precedes the word, in which the Spirit limits himself to proclaiming the Word. Hence a silence that is not simply the non-pronunciation of words, but a silence that contains the plenitude of all words and that spreads itself mysteriously.

And it is for this very reason that there must always be in the Church ministers of the Church divested of all human means—of culture, of wealth, of prestige, rich only in their indigence—the saintly parish priest of Ars can serve as model and patron—and also ministers whose *diaconia* is to observe silence and to transmit the experience through the ministry of silence. They are supreme witnesses of the Spirit and also serve as a reminder to the world and to Christians that in the domain of the things of God, only the Spirit is efficacious.

VI

There is must discussion in our post-conciliar time of renewal of the methods of priestly and religious formation. And that no doubt is an urgent and necessary task. No matter how high the level of the clergy is today as compared with other times of the Church, it is still very much this side of what it ought to be in order to respond appropriately to the present-day needs of the world, even more, those of the Spirit through the world. As a matter of fact, the more the structures of society are unable to weather the storm of an irresistible human evolution and disappear, the more the scaffoldings, buttresses and frameworks are swept away in the current of change, all the more must the Christian, and the priest essentially, situate himself and keep himself in the center. Not, of course, as though gathering oneself in this center in order to make a supreme effort to save structures or as though falling back on it in a military sense, abandoning the enjoined role of being the leaven in the world and the mission of divine presence among men, but by discovering in this very center the place from which the effulgence of God extends everywhere. Present in this center of self in which God dwells, he is by that very fact present to all the work of God; he acts everywhere with the efficacy of God, all his works are born of the Spirit.

As a matter of fact the renewal in progress in the seminaries and in the novitiates must lead to the discovery of this center by each one in one's own self, and not just to simple changes of programs and regulations. Is this not that very thing which seemed to inspire the Spirit when, in the course of the Council proceedings, he occasioned the request to be set forth that the formation of the clergy no longer be "monastic" and that instead it should conform more with the present-day needs of the priestly life in the world? To be sure, periods of silence and of "monastic" solitude are necessary to the priest and to Christians living in the world, just as the human organism requires periods of recuperative sleep for the proper performance of its functions. Periods of daily, weekly "retreat"—we think of the weekly day of silence and of fasting so dear to so many Hindus and to which Mahatma Ghandi strictly adhered—and, finally, of annual observances. However, what priests must above all move toward is to make certain that their presence to self and to the world should never make them lose the presence of God, even less should they be lost to artificial worked-up feelings of religious fervor. Rather, there should be a deepening of interior silence and a fixation of the soul on the inmost center where alone the soul possesses itself.[2]

Here it is not a question of a felt or conceived presence, but of a living presence that is not paired with their presence to the world. As long as the thought of God and the presence to self and to the world are felt as two different things, the Christian has not yet found his equilibrium in the Spirit. The priest is the minister and the witness of this presence in the world. He is the epiphany of the Presence of God in the universe and in each one of the consciousnesses that God has created in His image and in His likeness. He is the Great Vigil

Keeper in this world in the very mystery of his awakening to God in the depth of self, he is the Awakener by mission and by vocation. His essential ministry is to awaken souls to the Presence, for the hearing of the eternal Word.

Seen in this perspective, is not the essential work of formation in the seminaries and novitiates that of awakening one so deeply to this Presence that no distortion is any longer possible? If the Presence is simply thought or felt on the periphery of the soul, this thought or feeling will simply be one of the feelings or one of the thoughts that agitate the soul. They will inevitably conflict with the other feelings and thoughts that compete for the mind's attention and try to bend it in their direction. The Presence of God is recognized and the awakening to God, this experience of faith to which man is destined by his very birth in this world and marked by his baptismal character, is produced on a level having no common measure with all that is felt or thought. It is only at this level that the complete reversal of the soul, enjoined by the Gospel, is realized—the *metanoia* (repentance) that Jesus preached after John the Baptist and which Peter, in his turn, made the subject of his first public ministry on the day of Pentecost. This reversal, actually, is a passage from the "selfish center" of self to its profoundest and ultimate center wherein God dwells, where God truly becomes the principle of all our actions. Nor is it only a matter of acting for God, or of keeping the thought and desire of God in the first rank of the candidate's thought and desires. What is necessary, rather, is to effect total passage to the Breath of the Spirit.

Studies, disciplines, regulations, acquisition of good habits, all that is necessary, of course. Even more are scriptural readings, meditation and liturgical praise. Nevertheless, one dares say, all that is still only a means. The formation programs of the seminaries and of the novitiates must set their sights beyond that: they must aim at placing the soul in the presence of the living and true God whose presence is a consuming fire, they must aim to make each candidate feel the scorch of this Presence.

Any formation that does not aim at this ultimate goal is incomplete, if not dangerous. A minimum of love of God and of good will, perhaps, suffices to perform the peripheral tasks of the ecclesial *diaconia*. But the priest, of all persons, has no right to "sadden" the Spirit that dwells in him.

Let the priest before all else be the minister and the witness of the Presence, the awakener of souls to the inner mystery that calls them. Otherwise he risks being a burden for the Church and, more especially, for that portion of the flock that has been entrusted to him. In that case, as a matter of actual fact, he prevents the Spirit from raising him and from raising his own people and from carrying them, with his Breath of love, up to the Father who awaits them.

VII

Well, then, in that case, it might be objected, is it necessary that every priest, every religious should be a mystic?

Since in our day the term *mystic* has to accomodate itself in the most varied senses, according to the fantasy of writers, let us state quite clearly that in all truth and in actual fact, priests and religious should at least aim at being contemplatives.

What was said above certainly suffices to exclude unwarranted interpretations. What we understand by a contemplative attitude is, before all else, an ever increasingly profound attentiveness to the inner mystery, an opening to the silence of the Spirit beyond all feelings and all thought. If in the course of his formation the seminarian or the novice has acquired the conviction that the interior life consists essentially of thoughts or feelings on the subject of God, how will he be able later to be receptive to the touches of the Spirit which are rarely lacking when the soul acquires the habit of "self-communion"? And if he has never been invited to this "self-communion," how will he be able to keep his spiritual "self-communion," how will he be able to keep his spiritual life free of the distractions to which it is incessantly dragged by the world? It is necessary that the priest from the outset be initiated into the mystery of the Spirit within and that he learn how to make himself attentive to the voice of the Spirit, susceptible to his movement. The Spirit never fails to act in the docile soul, as St. Benedict insists in the seventh chapter of the Rule, and rightly so because that is what the Gospel itself teaches.

Moreover, can there be a real solidity of faith in the absence of this intimate experience? Present-day psychoanalysis early called into question the whole psychological apparatus of faith, whereas current philosophy sometimes subjects its rational base to examination. Faith takes root in the profound experience of a beyond, infinitely remote from all that can be perceived and felt. Admittedly this profound experience is most often unknown to the consciousness itself, but it is no less the effective support of this faith which psychology and dialectics try to breach. In that case, then, is it not normal that the Christian should try to integrate this experience into his very consciousness? Or, to put it more precisely, that he should deepen his level of consciousness so as to encounter in the depth of self this mystery which discloses itself to him only *per speculum in aenigmate?* And is it not, above all, the duty of the priest who must proclaim the faith to those who do not yet believe or who no longer believe, to nourish this faith—in an ever more abundant life—in those who already live of it?

The communist reproaches the Christian for his alienation. And recent dialogues have shown quite clearly the deep anguish felt by many profoundly sincere people vis-a-vis the Christian Churches, because it seemed to them that their acceptance of God would signify the negation of this mystery of conscience which they feel so strongly in their exercise of human freedom.[3]

What valid reply to the atheist communist could a Christian make who has not felt in the depth of his own self the experience of this *synergy* mentioned earlier, of this presence of God at the profoundest depth of man's being, of this springing up of human freedom in the profoundest depth of freedom and of the infinite love of God? Reason alone cannot go that far. Faith no doubt makes the Christian experience it, but faith as such aims at the illumination of the gift of intelligence and at the experience—*quasi per connaturalitatem* (St. Thomas)—of the gift of wisdom. The priest does not have a lived response to the most urgent problem of our time, namely atheism, if he has not, at least initially, undergone this experience, if, at the very least, he is not susceptible to it in the profoundest depth of his soul.

And even more, what valid and effective reply could the priest offer to the spiritual person in the Far East who on the one hand opposes the experience of the *tao* to his experience, and on the other, that of Buddha or of the Vedic *rishis?* For all these lofty wisdoms of Asia which to this very day still guide, from near or far, the spiritual life of a third of humanity, an intimate experience of the sources of being are at their very root.

To be sure the Christian faith has in itself the wherewithal to respond to all the questions posed by humankind. Indeed the role of the Church is to lead the whole world and each human being to his or her eschatological destiny. This role further requires that the Church must be willing to go ahead of the Spirit everywhere where the Spirit has chosen to wait for her and to arrange to meet her, in the heart of the sincere atheist and buddhist as well as in the heart of the Christian whom the contemporary discoveries of science and of human thought disquiet without let-up.

The solution of all these antinomies of the human spirit is found, without doubt, in the revealed mystery of the Trinity and of the reciprocal interiority of the Three divine Persons.

The Trinity, unfortunately, is too often presented to the Christian as an abstract concept, whereas it is the most concrete and most immediate reality that exists. But man must undergo the inmost experience of this reality of faith. He must discover in his own depth this reciprocal interiority of God and self. Indeed man was created in the image of God, of the Triune God. It is necessary that man discover himself ineffably, at one and the same time, as being of God and in God, on the model of the Son in whom he was created and in whom he lives. It is necessary that he *know,* beyond all thought and all feeling, that the Father calls him, in the eternal call of the Son, in the oneness of the Spirit.

That truly is this experience of God, this experience of Jesus-Man, of whom the priest has been constituted in the Church as the preeminent minister. For without this experience, at least inchoative in him, his ministry will remain superficial. To be sure he will usefully administer the sacraments, he will maintain the minimum level of Christian life among the souls in his charge. Nevertheless, no matter how brilliant his human qualities may be, he will be always incapable of leading souls to the Encounter for which they have been created. And he will be even more incapable of making those who remain outside the faith apprehend the call of God in the teachings of faith.

VIII

India turns her nose up at the knowledge which remains in the intelligence. She is interested only in the knowledge of life, that which leads to the inner mystery, that which completes the awakening within. India constantly resists the Greek temptation of the *eidos.* Whatever her infidelities and her deficiencies have been in the course of the ages, this flame has been unbrokenly maintained and its ideal always preserved at the highest level.

Teachers of the sciences and of philosophy instruct their pupils. The latter avidly gather what they teach, meditate on it and let it fructify in their minds.

The teacher of wisdom also teaches his disciples. He teaches them the *Vedas,* the other sacred texts, the examples of the saints. But he habituates them above all to penetrate to the profoundest depth of these texts, down to the very intuition from which they sprang up in the soul of the *rishi* who "heard" them. But only the one who has had a personal contact with the essential intuition can introduce the disciple, who listens to him and trusts him, to it. Only the one whose inner ear has known how to perceive the mystery of silence and to divine the barely perceptible signs that direct the mind in its inward quest, is capable of guiding the disciple to the secret of this silence, and to help him to perceive these signs.

The moment will then arrive in which he will no longer have anything to say to the disciple except: it is here. His last word has opened the last retreat of the heart of the disciple and provoked an awakening in him. But his last word, his final *mantra,* more than a barely audible whisper in the disciple's ear, will be a direct transmission from heart to heart, in the non-dual contact of the Spirit.

Such is the role of the guru of India. Such is the role also of the priest of the holy Church, at least such a priest as India understands and awaits.

The guru transmits the faith-experience of the sages of the Vedic times, an experience that he has made his own, under the guidance of his teacher.

The priest of the holy Church transmits the experience of the Lord Jesus, the *face to face* of the Father and of the Son in the non-duality of the Spirit. And every day he again finds the pledge and the sign of this experience in the celebration of the Sacrament. The Eucharist tends of itself to this plenitude of Spirit, *Spiritus pinguedinem.* The priest is not only the external minister of the sacrament, he is just as much the one who leads souls to the *realization* of this sacrament in the profoundest depth of their soul, up to an awakening to the Father in the Christ, in the love and oneness of the Spirit.

Such is the priest for whom India waits, for whom the world waits, for whom the Spirit waits, in the depth of the heart of India, in the depth of the heart of the world.

Who will hear the voice of the Spirit?

Chapter 6

Ghandi, Witness Of The Truth[1]

In 1939 India celebrated the centenary of the birth of Mohandas Karamchanda Gandhi. Manifestations in honor of the Mahatma took place almost everywhere else in the world. Gandhi, in fact, is not only a national figure in India. As a prophet, he belongs to the whole world. He is of the strain of those persons in whom the mystery of the invisible Presence has manifested itself in the midst of their brethren with a particularly intense brilliancy.

He was, of course, also a political personage, and his name is already inscribed in history as the liberator of his people. However, he was not only that, not even primarily that. Like many of his race, after and before him, he was one of those for whom this Presence was a living and felt reality, a Truth in which all life is rooted and which conditions all the activities of being. He loved to talk of a "little voice" that let itself be mysteriously heard in the depth of his heart and often declared that without an order from this voice, he never allowed himself to make a move—in the way Jesus constantly referred to the Father, to his voice, to his order, to his will.

This *little voice* was his way of referring to the interior Mystery, to this Presence, deepening and enveloping at once, to this inmost sense that would not permit him to live at the simple level of his senses, of his human reflection and of shifting circumstances. This mystery was his relationship, in the profoundest depths of his own self, with the world of the Absolute, of Eternity.

At the starting-point of his vocation, he was not so different from these sages who since time immemorial have risen in India's spiritual sky. Like them, he was fascinated by the *call from within*. But this interior call did not lead him, as was the case with so many others, to withdraw from the company of his fellows. In fact, he heard this call at a moment in which he experienced, and with particular anguish, the situation of his fellow-Indians both in South Africa, where he lived at that time, and in his homeland. Like Moses, he heard in his heart a voice that caused him to dedicate his life to the liberation of his people. Nevertheless, just like the leader of the tribes of Israel, he had never considered that winning freedom for his people was first of all and, necessarily, a means of recovering its soul in constant danger of sinking into sloth in a state of bondage and under the foreign yoke.

For him national liberation was only a stage toward inner freedom. And the means to obtain this political liberation were by themselves already exercises of inner liberation in his thought and in his will. The times of rebellion against an authority without an authentic mandate were moments that would forge souls for the times to come. Hence the weapons of non-violence, so difficult to utilize, which were the only ones he put in the hands of his companions: Non-cooperation, *ahimsa, satyagraha.*

Before fighting against the enemy without and the enemy in others, it was necessary first of all to fight in one's inmost self the one and only enemy who, wherever he may be, is falsehood and selfishness, hatred and violence, greed for what belongs to others. Contrary to most revolutionaries, he preached love of the opponent. He did not hesitate for a moment to call a halt to a movement of non-cooperation in progress upon perceiving that his companions were being carried away by passion and that the movement was turning to hatred and violence.

He rejected all hatred, no matter against whom it was

directed. Only evil can and must be hated, he said. And first
of all the evil in one's own self. As long as some hatred remains in the heart, the struggle is unjust.

It is only in love and in truth that man has the right to oppose his brother man. And to refuse to do so when justice
demands it would be just as great a sin against truth. For if
truth liberates, as Christ teaches, it permits no one to retire
within his or her bourgeois and selfish smugness.

Christ also said that he had not come to bring to the earth a
cowardly and selfish peace but, on the contrary, to bring to
the world a liberating dissension and a sword. No one more
than Ghandi has put into practice the Johannine formula: *to
do the truth.* He called his movement of non-violence and
non-cooperation *satyagraha. Satyagraha* is the ascendancy of
truth, the attachment to truth without mincing words or com-
promise, the consecration of the whole being to this truth.
For him, Truth was the loftiest name that human beings
could give to God. What Christian can forget that Jesus came
into the world precisely in order to bear witness to the Truth
and that this witness led him to the Cross—the same cross to
which he calls his followers.

Gandhi won political independence for his country as the
result of his consecration, and the consecration of his
followers, to Truth. And free India adopted as her motto the
ancient upanashadic mantra: *satyam eva jayate,* "Truth
always prevails."

To be sure Gandhi had his peculiarities which amused or
annoyed his followers. No doubt some of his options can be
debated; no doubt free India, on the whole, still remains
quite far from the lofty ideal that Ghandi would have liked to
inculcate in her soul. Nevertheless it was precisely this
idealism of Ghandi, this sense of the Absolute, of the Truth,
of Love, that he derived from his contemplation of the inner
mystery, his sense, in a word, of the sovereign Presence of
God, which shook and drew this people, which made it attach

itself to the Mahatma as to a charismatic leader, as to an emissary of God, and to follow him blindly in defiance of all obstacles. This people recognized itself in him.

Ghandi's spirit is latent in the heart of this people, even if it does not shine as much as one would like it to. The call heard by Ghandi was not exceptional in India. What was exceptional was Ghandi's response to this call. This call is always there and even the response is not lacking for the Indian who is sufficiently attentive. There is always a Vinoga in India, the truest perhaps of all of Ghandi's disciples. And there are also many humble people scattered a little everywhere in our cities and villages of whom no one speaks and who influence the apparent destiny of their country only slightly, but who guard its soul. The Spirit ever breathes.

Many Christians reproach Ghandi for not having joined the Church. Some dared even to accuse him of insincerity. Had he not read the Bible? Had he not loudly proclaimed that the figure and the message of Christ had exercised a great influence on him?

His failure to take this step may have been precisely due to the fact that Ghandi was too attached to truth, to this very truth that Jesus preached, to arrive at recognizing in the Church the authentic and unique messenger of this truth. One cannot exaggerate the obstacle that the life of too many Christians of the East and of the West creates to the spread of the gospel message in our India. Not, of course, because it occasions direct scandal. But does not its very mediocrity deprive it of its right to bear witness to Christ in the eyes of those who take the truth of the Gospel in total seriousness?

Perhaps it can be attributed also, and above all, to this sense of the absolute of God which is at the base of the whole religious attitude of India? God is beyond all expression, all form, all history. Saints and prophets all manifest him, each in his own way. Each one is the mystery of God become visible among men. The current of the river returns to its source, the manifestation to the manifested, the form to the mystery that goes beyond all form, time to eternity. Attentive to God everywhere, the sage discovers him everywhere. All signs lead him to Him. And he sees no reason to give privileged preference to one or the other of these signs. To the signs of his tradition that he had received as a child, Ghandi freely added new signs which new circumstances brought to his attention. But the new signs themselves always lead back to the old signs in his soul. The name that above all he liked to give to God was the one that he had learned to murmur as a child: *Rama,* the Beautiful One, the Beloved One. *Ram, Ram,* these were the last syllables that his dying lips breathed out. How could God not have heard them and received him?

For the Christian Ghandi's vocation (like that of his great contemporaries—an Aurobindo, a Ramana Maharashi) is a source of joy, but also one of infinite sadness. Of joy and, indeed, of an immense joy because God has spread his graces with such abundance as far as the Gentiles even before they had learned to invoke the revealed names of the Savior and above all to give Him their faith. But it is also a source of sadness, for does not the Christian greatly and devoutly desire that all souls—and above all the greatest souls—come to the direct knowledge of the mystery of salvation and that all join their voice to the canticle that the Universe sings to the Redeemer Lamb, in the communion of the holy Church?

The mystery is a great one as a matter of fact because the spiritual radiance of India in the world—we mean the true radiance which has nothing to do with trade and propaganda—still passes more through the sages and saints of the Hindu tradition than through their eschatological heirs who should be the Christians of India, the official disciples of Jesus . . .

Whatever the case may be, Ghandi is among those, Christians and others, who left everything for God; he is of the race of Thérèse of Lisieux who a few hours before dying confided: "I have ever searched only for truth." If it be permitted to conclude by suggesting to Christians some practical applications of Ghandi's example, could not one say that the present-day disputants with things as they are should carefully mediate his message and his attitude of soul—we are thinking, of course, of the disputants within the Church, but more of those whose very fidelity to the Gospel make them opponents of unjust socio-economic or political systems. Even when these revolutionary Christians decide to resort to direct action, they must always remember that while the truth, at times, authorizes recourse to the sword—to defend their oppressed brethren—the heart must always preserve itself absolutely pure. The last resort of Christian revolutionary movements can be nothing else but love and truth.

That God has availed himself of a *Gentile* to recall this to humankind is only one of His mysteries.

Chapter 7

"In Tamil Nadu
God Is The Child"[1]

Spiritual Childhood and Upanishad

It is common in the Indian tradition to compare the state of perfection with that of the child; in the State of Tamil Nadu, even more energetically, one says: God is the child. It would certainly be worthwhile if an Indian devotee of St. Thérèse of Lisieux would make an inventory of the texts that refer to spiritual childhood. Here I shall limit myself to the presentation of a text from the *Brihad-aranyaka-Upanishad* (3,5) which has often impressed me during the course of my readings. My translation may be somewhat loose, but I am convinced that it will not betray the author's thought and also that it will transmit the essential teaching of the sacred text more clearly to the ordinary reader.

"In the course of a discussion about *brahman* (the ultimate Principle, the Absolute at once immanent and transcendent to all that which is) the priest Kahola asked rishi Yajnavalkya:

—Yajnavalkya, could you explain to me very exactly what is this brahman who is immediately present to us, who cannot escape our consciousness (literally "our eyes") this *atman* (this "spirit", this "soul", this "self") who is the very soul of all that which exists?—

—It is your very own *atman,* who is in all that is.—

—What sort of *atman,* precisely, who is in all that is?—

Yajnavalkya does not reply right then with a definition. The last mystery does not allow for definitions. All the teacher can ever do is to direct the gaze of the disciple on what he wants him to see. It is the disciple himself, with his own eyes, who must discover that which the teacher can at best point out to him. Moreover, are not such questions about the *atman* and the *brahman* equivalent to asking at full noon what is this light that fills all and makes all visible?

As an experienced teacher Yajnavalkya therefore simply tries to open Kahola's eyes inwardly.

> —That which (in you, in all) is beyond hunger and thirst, suffering, aging and death—that, Kahola, this 'self'. When the wise man has recognized it, then he no longer feels any desire, neither for lineage, nor for wealth, nor for any world that be (here below or beyond), for that is only desire. Let the wise man then renounce knowledge and become like a child. Then let him abandon childhood as well as knowledge and become a *mouni*! Finally, equally indifferent to being a *mouni* or not being one, he will become a *brahman* (an authentic knower of *brahman*).
> —Yajnavalkya, how then will be become *brahman?*
> —Simply in becoming one, Kahola!''

In the commentary on the Brahman-sutras (3,4, 50), Shankara asks himself what must exactly be understood by this state of childhood. Is it the freedom from care of the child who freely and blindly follows his instincts and impressions? No, he replies; what characterizes (spiritual) childhood is the absence of malice and of vanity. The child has no idea of acting as though he were a "big shot," so to speak, and of displaying his talents and worth—the very opposite of what the upanishad calls *pandityam,* the satisfaction of knowing and of showing off this knowledge. The child is simply itself

without a look at what it is and why it is. Nor does the child
look back to ponder the matter.

The Vedantic ascesis can be defined as a return to the
beginnings, to that innate state in us which is not reached by
the process of becoming and which cannot be touched by the
changes that the successive conditions of existence produce in
our body and our mind. Return to the beginnings? More exactly still, it is the discovery of that which is in us beyond all
lived, thought or felt beginning. Even when the adult has
recognized this inmost mystery of his being, does he not try
constantly to formulate it, to *reach* it, whereas *that* is also as
immediately present to him as the light to his eyes and the air
to his lungs?

It is no doubt the child's total transparence to itself,
beyond all reflection, that further strikes Indian thought
when it reflects on the state (more than on the way or path) of
spiritual childhood—at least at the level of the way of wisdom
or *Jnana;* for the tradition of the *bhakti* (loving devotion) will
certainly be sensitive to the attitude of trust and self-
surrender to fatherly love which has been so solidly developed
by the saint of Lisieux.

Nevertheless the upanishad loves analysis, paradox, indefinite progressions—for is it not constantly necessary to
wrest man away from all that in which he tends ineluctably to
come to a stop, to become smug, in the course of the
journey? The loftiest and the sublimest still being an obstacle
on the path that leads to that which is beyond all measure.

One would think in fact that all had been said once the
ideal of the child had been proposed. Not at all! Indeed it is
necessary to renounce being a child as well as a savant and to
become a *mouni* (or: a silent one, or: the one who is led by
the interior inspiration) after which it is necessary to abandon
all interest in being or not being a silent or an inspired one.
Only then does one become a true sage, the one who knows
through inward experience the very mystery of *brahman* and

who in his whole being is nothing else but the pure radiance of this unique *brahman.*

Some commentators, among them Shankara himself in another treatise, cannot accept that the upanishad should propose a state higher than that of childhood; for this reason they do violence to the text and try to read *balya* (short a) for "strength" instead of *bâlya* for "childhood." This once more proves the importance of the Indian tradition as regards the supreme value of the state of childhood in spiritual life.

A very simple explanation, moreover, can be given for the antinomy. The child is unconscious of its freedom from care and of its freedom. It does not think that it acts as a child. But the adult who again becomes a child finds it hard to forget that he has returned to childhood. And he becomes again an adult in the very formulation of his state of childhood: it is the same with the one who is in silence. When he becomes conscious that he has attained this silence of inwardness, he has already broken this silence and is no longer a *mouni.* At the level of the ultimate experience, of perfect childhood and of total silence, it is as though that which could be said of wisdom, of childhood and of silence has evaporated, and nothing else remains but the *brahman,* alone and without second. The crystal that reflects the light is so one with the light that it no longer knows anything neither of itself nor of the light. . . .

There is no word to utter this mystery; there is no act conducive to arriving at it. *That is,* quite simply, just as the child is, and it is itself without thinking upon it.

"I tell you solemnly, anyone who does not welcome the kingdom of God like a little child will never enter it!"

PART TWO

Unpublished Excerpts From The

Correspondence Of Henri Le Saux

/Swami Abhishiktananda

1948-1973

TO MADAME L. CHARNELET

>Shantivanam
>Saccidananda Ashram
>June 7, 1958

The more I live . . . the more I feel that this ideal of pure contemplation and of living the indigence of Indian life form the absolutely indispensable condition for a real development of the Church in this country.

No doubt the Lord will have His hour for making everything understood; while waiting, it suffices to be the silent reminder of what can be. The transmission of the word of God is a work of the Spirit, and the external works which do not plunge deeply into the depth of the soul where the Spirit dwells will remain vain and useless. Contemplation—true contemplation and not simple piety—is the most important ministry of the Church, today above all. Oh! how much more so here where religious India judges the bearers of a spritual message not by their words nor by their achievements, but by the witness which they themselves give of the life in the depths of the Spirit.

Henri Le Saux

Shantivanam
Saccidananda Ashram
September 30, 1958

The devotion to St. Thérèse is widespread here. In the Tamil language they call her the "Little Flower" (in Tamil *Pushpai*) and many bear this name. But what draws the monk even more to her is the life of divestment and interior nakedness that was hers. And it is this way beyond the senses and the mind that is the way of India. The Church does not sufficiently display to India her real riches, and precisely those that would attract the Hindu.

May prayers be said in Lisieux asking that the Carmelite Order in India be truly radiant with the spirituality of St. John of the Cross. The more I live, the more I think—perhaps I have already touched on this—that what is most lacking in the Church of India is a profoundly contemplative spirituality, based on St. John of the Cross and Tauler (whom St. Thérèse loved to quote) etc.

I remain solitary in this ashram which is too big for me. But who will ever get to know anything whatsoever about this inner mystery if he has not savoured of this solitude within and without? May the Lord guide the future as He sees fit. If it be His discretion to send a "change of guard" may He send *steely* vocations. This will be a miracle of the first magnitude. May St. Thérèse send them to us for the development of the Church of India and the radiance of Christ the Lord.

. . . . .

Shantivanam
January 14, 1959

Madame,
I received your letter around Christmas and I thank you. You know that I received a letter from Lisieux that went

straight to my heart. To send such encouraging messages into
the course of a solitary journey are the tactful attentions of
Providence. It is one more proof that the Shantivanam is in
the line willed by God. What matters what humans may think
of it, and what matters the absence of external success! The
will of the Lord in regard to Shantivanam is without doubt
this solitary and hidden advance. One more proof, in our so
scattered and exteriorized time, that the works of God are
wrought in silence and through the work of inwardness much
more than through external activism. The transformation of
the world will never be anything else than a work of grace.
And grace must be sought for in the profoundest depth of
self, for the world as for one's self. Such is the role of contemplatives. May God make all the "contemplatives" of the
world be "contemplatives" in actual fact.

TO MOTHER FRANÇOISE-THÉRÈSE OF THE INFANT JESUS[1] OF THE CARMELITE ORDER OF LISIEUX

Indore
May 18, 1959

Reverend Mother,

I have been living here (Indore) for several days with a
young Hindu man of Delhi who has given up his worldly circumstances etc. in order to live here in solitude and contemplation. We feel extremely close to each other. But the
more I meet the best among the Hindus, the more insoluble
appears to me the problem of making them accept Christ just
as He is. He too was reminded this morning that the contemplative presence is the only means for presenting Christianity, as a spiritual life, to India. The rest will never touch
the Hindu soul in its depths. . . . Alas! how is one to make it
understood in the Church that we have no need of "technique" here, but of authentic mystics, of contemplation: it is

for the Lord to make this understood and to make the call to the desert heard in the depth of the heart of the Christians of India.

I received with great joy the manuscripts and the letters, in Indore. How kind of you. I also read with deep emotion the account of the last days of Mother Geneviève and of the life of Mother Jeanne. Blessed be the Lord. May the spirit of true contemplation thus remain in Lisieux.

Let us remain present to the essential Presence, faithful to the Spirit, letting him lead us; it is not necessary to know whence the Spirit comes, whither the Spirit goes. But what is essential is to be docile!

In this essential Presence.

Henri Le Saux

Shantivanam
October 26, 1959

Reverend Mother,

I have found in Indore, to my great joy, the envelope that contained the reliquary, your letter and the good news about the novitiate. And, as a bonus, the volumes of St. John of the Cross. How all that makes one "feel good." The Lord often suppresses all consolations and then, quite simply, by touches of this kind of His love, He makes one understand that He is there and that He leads all.

I have just returned to the *Shantivanam* and, captivated anew by the charm of this solitude, I now find the appeals coming from the North, their urgency notwithstanding, burdensome. Will the Lord at last listen to all these prayers that are being said and asking for a blossoming of vocations to the ideal of the SVN in France and in India at one and the same time? Ought I confess that I am, no doubt, the one who prays less for that intention? Is there not a place in the soul in which "asking" no longer makes any sense? Why spend one's time in "informing" the Lord, said a Quaker friend to me recently. Martha, you worry and fret about so many things. However, I would be quite content if the Lord should send a change of the guard. To be sure, this vocation is Carmelite, but it is also Carthusian, Benedictine, Franciscan. Human beings make all these distinctions. There are ways through which the Lord lets each one rise to life and in which He aids each one, depending on whether one truly feels capable of going the whole way and orients himself or herself accordingly. Then each one says: "My way is the best." Now, ultimately, ways are valid only for the purpose of leading to the "non-way." What trace does a bird leave in the sky?, asked Job. As long as there are ways, one *delights* in one's chosen way and one fashions a Lord to one's measure . . . and stops at his or her peace, and stops at *his* or *her* joy over belonging to the Lord, as if it were not the very "joy of the Lord" himself in which we must enter—if indeed one has ever left it. For what is there outside the bosom of the Father? Liturgies, of course, are necessary to the world. But what the world needs even more are Franciscans of the first hour, people who take St. Francis and, therefore, Jesus literally without playing the role of the one who understands the situation better than did the saints and who composes editions of the Gospel and of the primitive Rules. They are the wandering Christians for whom India awaits. Perhaps, however, the Carmelite Order, at least such as I idealize it in my vision, is what in the Church is closest to India's profoundest tendency: the a-cosmic attitude of the Fathers of the desert: "Flee, be quiet, lie still" of St. Arsenius, the "nada" of St. John of the Cross, the passage beyond all things, Tauler's and Eckhart's establishment of self beyond self. It is that which the Christian monk must live in the company of his *advaitin* brother, if he truly wants to *complete* in Christ the intuition of the being of the *Saccidananda** of the India of the *rishis*. And the completion in *Christo* of the *advaitin* mystical intuition is the primordial ontological condition for the establishment (not through statistics, nor through gim-crack buildings, but *in re*) of the Church in India. That is essentially the aim and the role of the monk of *Saccidananda*. Perhaps it was not strongly spelled out in *Ermites***, the first draft of which appeared in 1950/51, followed by the French adaptation in 1953. At that time I saw things more in the traditional frames, whereas I would now see the realization of Christian life more in the form of Egypt and of what obtains here: the guru, the abbot simply with some disciples whom he forms and who in their turn will swarm like bees. I fear insitu-tionalization more than ever. However, and I stated this clearly in *Ermites,* I have envisaged the Benedictine life as practiced by me and one which on the other hand is so flexi-ble, as a point of departure and practically as a necessity for the central *ashram* of formation, leaving the path wide open for further swarms. The Lord will show through cir-cumstances themselves what is to be done if one day He wills that SVN be magnified. One does not put new wine in old goatskin bottles. There are only analogies between the forms of the East and those of the West. Indian Christian monasticism will also be *sui generis.* One must also go beyond present-day Western Christian forms. What are needed here are Indian editions, lived in flesh and spirit, of the Little Way of St. Theresa of Avila, of St. John of the Cross, not copies or renewals thereof. A daughter should resemble her mother, but go beyond her mother, be herself and not her mother.

---

*God, Tr.

**The reference is to *Ermites du Saccidananda,* an essay on the Christian integra-tion of India's monastic tradition. See list of published works of Fr. Le Saux, p. ¥ Tr.

You will tell all that to Sister Thérèse of Jesus,* the head-mistress of the novices. If she so desires, I'll write her further another time by ordinary mail. It is a joy to pray in *union* with this novitiate of Lisieux and to pray that it *continue* the mission of Lisieux, a mission that is not simply to transmit the Little Way, but to live it and to make it live in new cir-cumstances of time and place, as it is rightly expressed in the *Annales* dedicated to Mother Geneviève, pages that are so stirring and that stem from a time whose *point of view* is often no longer ours. May the two Theresas quicken Christian-Indian contemplation in India. There are thoroughgoing fervent souls in our Carmelite Orders and some who have understood. But what would be necessary here are Carmelite Orders freed of many forms of detail—and while safeguarding their solitude, still in *contact* with India. There are some ideas on this subject here or there but which "visitor" will understand?

I shall send the book to Japan this week. Don't fail to tell me to send the book wherever it can be useful, and I shall do so with great pleasure.

There are two beautiful texts in *Morceaux choisis.*[1] And that proves that the Spirit blows *everywhere.* In Gospel times, there were already people who expelled demons in the name of Jesus without being of the Twelve. Christ is present everywhere, even where his name is not yet "known," and the Spirit everywhere prepares his *advaitin* advent—among men, things and human groups.

In a union of prayer through fidelity to the vocation of Presence, in the Presence of God and in the name of man; in

---

*Head-mistress of the novices in the Carmelite Order of Lisieux, who left for In-dia in 1965. After spending several years in the Carmelite Order of Pondicherry, she obtained authorization to lead an eremetic life in northern India on the banks of the Ganges. She died in September of 1976, probably from drowning in the Ganges.

the presence of man and in the name of God. The Son and the Father behold each other, and what else is there?

Shantivanam
November 14, 1959

Reverend Mother,

I learned yesterday, through the letter of Sister Thérèse of Jesus, of the call to the House of the Lord of your good and pious M____ in order to receive the Lord under his ____ illed her that morning to an eternal ____ veil!

____ther's glory is sung by the whole ____ through the whole universe He sings ____ anticle of His Word. Are we so out ____ ut of the divine filiation that we in- ____ it would no longer be true? The ____ ndition to the other is but an acci- ____ the mystery of the Reality that we ____ , Jesus thrice recalls to the Jews: ____ ? Death cannot touch this divine ____ lepth of my selfhood.

ABHISHIKTANANDA

Shantivanam
December 29, 1959

____ which the ideal of Saccidanan-
d____ in India and in the Church (by means of Christian India). And the Lord has need of that since He wills to make use of man and in our era of techniques (which invade even the Church), the inaction of India must be there in order to counter-balance western and, above all, far western activism. Inaction, in the Church, is gratuitous contemplation and the acceptance of simply being there. In the past weeks I

was thinking that total solitude is marvelous and ultimately easy providing one does not try to compensate for the absence of human community by substitutes (in fact or in desire, and under beautiful pretexts): receiving or making visits, studying, writing, reading. All that is well, but in the case of a contemplative it is not a remedy. His role is different. His role is non-role and his function non-function. He is in the world the witness of God, and of that which in God defies all expression, all manifestation of God in so far as He is outside of all reach, etc. And before God, he is the witness that man has accepted that God is truly the beyond. It suffices to God that he "remain there;" and the one for whom that does not suffice has understood nothing of his "call" to solitude. If God wills to make use of him in the world of man, it is up to God to let him know it. And in so far as the "inspiration" to act, to write, to study, to found "things" is not clear beyond doubt, the solitary ought not budge . . . All the failures are not such in actuality if through them Shantivanam may discover its proper self; as long as man wills to act concurrently with the Spirit, what can the Spirit do? So if God wills to make use of him notwithstanding, he must be reduced to helplessness. Nights are as irreplaceable for institutions as for human beings . . .

Pondicherry
February 3, 1960

Reverend Mother,

I have received your two successive letters in Pondi, where I am in the hospital. You must have at the same time received the letter that I wrote you last week before the operation. Everything transpired admirably, the kindness of everybody involved, doctors, sisters (from Cluny), nurses and others multiplying the efficacy of the treatment. I have to remain in bed for only a few more days, then a stay of a few days in

Pondi and, between the 14th and the 17th, I shall return to Shantivanam. It is a very instructive experience in physical helplessness and one which teaches you to bless the Lord no less when one is bed-ridden or on one's feet, when one cannot drink or be slaked to one's fill, and the rest . . . The manifestations of His love are multiple, but there is nothing that is not a manifestation of His love. And the works or acts that we perform are multiple, but all that is only the multiform expression of the unique act: to be of Him, to be in His Presence, to be in Him, to be quite simply . . .

More profoundly, there are two tendencies: the one to remain seated in the presence of the Lord, or better, hidden in Him—the other to reveal this secret to those who are awaiting perhaps only ? word in order to open themselves . . . I confess that for quite a long time I have been drawn by both. Finally, I believe that the monk ought to be "silent" until the Lord beckons him with sufficient clearness to "murmur" the secret of silence, according to the magnificent utterance of St. Ignatius of Antioch that you recalled to me the other day: "Come to the Father". The Word is born of Silence. And the Spirit who proceeds from the Word and from the Silence can say *Come to the Silence* . . .

I'll be returning to the SV for St. Benedict's day, and the anniversary will be feted in all inwardness but with no guests. But a great and profound thanksgiving will rise to the Lord for everything that He has done in these twenty years. All was grace. All has been *valde bonum*. As I said in my last letter, were someone to feel the call to the life of solitude within and without, what a grace! I must have told you about this dream of the "The Laura of the Himalayas" which would extend to the mountain all along the branches of the Ganges which are places of pilgrimages. When the Lord "will call," He will reduce the obstacles on the road, as foretold in Isaiah.

The life of solitude normally demands *at the beginning* a
rather strict use of time and a work of a sufficiently absorbing character. Other experiences have confirmed my own, but
I believe that one must liberate oneself from that as soon as
possible. It seems to me that the hermit normally ought
always to be free, ever available for prayer. To ward off the
temptation of idleness it would, perhaps, be enough for him
to have a serious work at his disposal. I mean to say a serious
reading demanding application of mind and to which he can
devote himself when he is not in form to remain retired within
himself. You know the ancient formula, transmitted especially by the Benedictine tradition, of the *lectio divina*. That is
what should be the hermit's normal occupation. This is the
requisite for a durable life of solitude.

For a retreat? The retreat is not a time to inform oneself
about God through reading, nor for informing God through
explicit petitional prayers, thanksgiving etc. (These formulas
came to me from an English Quaker friend). They seem
highly suggestive, or at least this applies to the retreats of
contemplatives. I would say it is a time to listen to God, to
collect oneself in His Presence, to forget oneself, to acquire
new strength in His veritable nature (Tauler's super-essence),
according to the expression that I love, in order simply *to be*.
This is what I said to a native of Kashmir who came to Shantivanam two years ago. He looked at me with an astonished
air and several days later he told me of his amazement at
simply "being." And for a Christian this simple word has
even deeper, more marvelous resonances than for the Hindu.

Three years ago I spent five weeks in total solitude in a
locked room, receiving my meals through a tower. It was
built *ad hoc* by some Hindu friends who make annual so-
journs there (one of them spends three or four months in it
without interruption), and the only reading matter I had was
the New Testament in Latin and some upanishadic excerpts. I
read but little of them using them above all for the purpose of

finding the more relevant texts. If one accepts, totally, if one embraces, if one hugs this solitude, this silence of the books, this very silence of inward speculation, with all one's heart, with no mental reservation, without trying to create a substitute, it seems to me that the "lotus" is bound to open itself in an already interiorized soul. The more the days go by, the more all seems far, far away and the essential alone remains. Nothing is understood nor seen (I mean within) for that would be precisely the source of the danger for psychically weak souls. The emptiness would be affected.

The Christian kneels to pray, the Hindu seats himself down in a way so that the body is immobilized as much as possible, so that the breathing abates, so that the mental whirl slows down, so that the mind centers itself and, by so doing, penetrates this "profoundest center" in which it has trespassed. This is not to be copied literally, but is it not a suggestive aid for going beyond oneself in the Son, and with the Son going even further beyond oneself to the beginning, to the principle, to the bosom of the Father. . . ? Our intelligence will never know this place that is essentially "ours" save in the faith here below. Probing it theologically is all very well, but why be afraid to abandon one's mind to this emptiness, to this going beyond self where, assuredly, no notion will come to satisfy the mind (but what notion does not betray God and does not betray our true being?), but where mysteriously and plenitudinously, one "is."

In the joy of Being

   a Patre, per Filium in Spiritu

                              ABHISHIKTANANDA

Shantivanam
February 3, 1960

True suffering is measured by our distance from God or
His proximity, which is all one. For God is too near for one
to be able to embrace Him or even to behold Him or even to
prostrate oneself before Him. That I think will be—is—the
true form of the "Night" of India. The Greek and the whole
West is constricted by its conceptualization when it fixes its
gaze on God. God does not adhere to our ideas of God. And
the theologian has more to suffer than anyone else when God
calls to him in the deepest and inmost recesses of his own self.
Here the God of Revelation does not oppose reason but He
seems to oppose, if I dare say so, this experience "that in His
profoundest depth I am no other." That is the Night of India. I have said "seems to oppose" in a first approximation
for, quite to the contrary, it is a deeper penetration of this
very experience. It is as though the Spirit has been touched
first of all in his mystery of being "Love," the bond, the
Union of the Two, the Person without "face," the one who
proceeds, as theology insists, from the Father and from the
Son *qua* "One." Then, in the faith in the words of Jesus, the
mystery of the "non-two" half-opens, being discloses its last
secret, the Spirit reveals the Father and the Son. And the
soul, wholly remaining in its real experience, divines that this
"I" that springs up from its profoundest depth is the
marvelous exchange of the reciprocal and inseparable I-Thou
of the Father and of the Son . . . and in the Son, the soul remains hidden. This is the mystery of the Resurrection. *I am
risen and I am evermore with Thee.* The soul has found itself
again, it has recovered the *face to face,* but without losing
anything of the marvelous unity of the Spirit that was given
to it from the outset. But all that is faith, stark, naked faith. I
had to tell you this, that it is necessary for this essential night
of India to be lived within the souls of the consecrated so that

India, in the depths of her being may half-open itself to this faith and hear the Spirit murmur to her: Come to the Father. Christian India must be born—a birth that is a resurrection—in the "depth" in order to be able "to appear."

To be sure this way of envisaging the mission and the mystery of India is mystical in every sense. And the one whose eye is not open inwardly will find it difficult to distinguish appearances from actualities . . . .

. . . Without doubt this takes place neither within nor without, and prayer always remains when one has grasped that there is nothing else but sign, reflection and manifestation of the Lord. Nevertheless the ministry of silence and of prayer is irreplaceable. And what is essential, as you say, is to preserve absolutely the first and foremost place for interior silence. And I know through experience how difficult that is.

Pondicherry
February 24, 1960

In the SV, at the beginning of May, I'll be receiving a group of non-Catholics (four or five denominations, most of them, if not all, "priests"), for a week of prayer and studies. That can be very fruitful in helping these brothers find the path to "interior" prayer and contemplation again. Among them there are also various yearnings and capacities for receptiveness. The two friends (an Anglican, a Presbyterian) who arranged this gathering are, moreover, of an admirable humility desiring only to learn and to receive. It is through the depth that "the" churches will again find their unity, just as it is through the depth that India and the Church will meet.

I do not say to you union in prayer, but union in silence, in the profoundest depth.

For what is to be asked for?

After all, is HE not?

And what place for any kind of desire is there in the one

who has "groped" his or her way through the smallest bit of that . . . ?

ABHISHIKTANANDA

Shantivanan
November 16, 1961

Everything is simple from the moment that one has grasped quite simply that God is Father and that one *is* only in Him. All is love and all is divine generation and all is response to this divine generation of love. All is light and there is no shade in the effulgence of the Trinity. It suffices merely to behold it. Men bestir themselves and the Lord makes use of them in order to realize His Christ. And He rightly shows how after all He has no need of us. He plays tricks on us or He forces us to rest, or He simply calls us to Paradise (like Father François de Sainte-Marie)[1] just when we think that we may still have something to do for Him. Time counts for so little. The only important thing is to rejoin eternity in the present instant, to center oneself in the very process of the generation of the Son of God, springing up in the eternal instant from the bosom of the Father and nevertheless fixed in it for eternity. And I believe that it is truly there that man works in real earnest. It is in the "heart" of man, of Christ, of the Father, in the *guha*, in the crypt of the heart, that the Church is born and grows, that the faith spreads and that grace is transmitted. It is in and through these mystical sources that the Sacrament obtains its total efficacy. But who agrees to work only in the divine generation? Or, at least, to work therein *first* and *foremost,* the rest being efficacious only in the measure that one manifests, expresses and radiates this mystery of inwardness?

In the joy of the Lord always. As St. Paul says to the Romans (chapter 8), what can separate me from the love of the Lord? Since all is His love and since all is the final offer-

ing of the Son to the Father, the response to this love.
In the oneness of the Spirit, the "bond" of the Trinity.

Shantivanam
January 14, 1962

. . . After all what do the details of life matter, health or
sickness, peace or war, and all these *davandvas* (dualities, op-
positions), as we say here! There is only one reality, the call
of love from the Father, the response of love that the Son
gives in the oneness of the Spirit. That I always repeat, but it
is not the essential thing. Through all these means the Lord
tries to release in us all the possibilities of a filial response that
He has put in our hearts in creating us. Our only aim is the
eternal chant of *Abba Pater* in the Son, the deification, as the
Fathers of the East said. For who, if not God, can say to
God: *Thou, my Father.* And in Jesus the impossible was ac-
complished: we are sharers in the divine nature; it is St. Peter
who says it. Then it is necessary that the Lord come to seek us
in the furthermost recesses of our being, at that point where
we try to escape Him, to be ourselves alone, even under the
marvelous pretext that He needs us and that we must serve
Him. It is necessary that He dislodge us from everywhere so
that the Spirit may remain all alone everywhere in us, for as
long as there remains in us something that has not passed to
the deification, to the mystery of the Son, there is something
in us that cannot yet cry *Abba Pater.* It is necessary that the
Lord immerse us into this nothingness of creation from which
we are drawn and that there be naught else but "the one who
lives for God, in God." Did not Jesus, even though He was
God, immerse himself in the agony and in the dereliction of
the Cross? It was necessary, says St. Paul, that He "learn"
obedience in his human nature . . . Therefore wherever we
may be, whatever He may demand of us, when He reduces us
to helplessness, when our efforts for Him remain without the

least apparent result . . . joy, not only notwithstanding all
that, but precisely for that. He is! what else do we want? And
He is, and He manifests that He is in all that. *Cantate
Domino canticum novum quia mirabilia fecit.* Judas,
Caiaphas and Pilate were the instruments of such
mirabilia . . .

Shantivanam
September 28, 1962

The Carmelite Order is so much more profound than any
particular manifestation of its ideal. Saints are never anything
else but signs and invitations from the Lord to go to the
depths of one's own self. To stop and look at them to excess
is to act like the bibliophile for whom a book's binding and
typography count infinitely more than the content. . .

So you see, what's important in the Church and
everywhere is to be sufficiently "deep" in order to transcend
the letter, which does not mean to "reject" it. The crucial
problems find their solution only in the deepening of "self."

In the joy of the Lord

Shantivanam
October 25, 1962

The contemplative, of course, must not be *tied* to the
Eucharist. But for as long as the Lord accords us the
Eucharist, we would be greatly in the wrong not to profit
from it fully. We are human beings and we need signs, and
the nearness of the tabernacle helps us to realize the interior
nearness, a nearness that is so immediate that one can no
longer realize it except as an object placed opposite our eyes.
See the *Invitatory* of Corpus Christi which is so significant.

This question of "rest," some day I would like to know
just what you are alluding to, what methods etc. I confess

that I myself have not found the solution. Nevertheless I would have a fair amount of possibilities at my disposal, from both a Christian and a Hindu point of view, for mastering "fatigue." Fatigue perhaps depends before all else on the mind's incessant mental whirl. The exercise of mental emptiness (directly, or with the aid of very brief formulas concentrating the attention on *one* point, for example, the Jesus Prayer—personally I make use rather of *Abba Pater*) seems essential to me (breath control is advisable in this regard). Then, secondarily, *a total liberation from "concern for self."* This ought to be so easy for the "consecrated" who no longer have any familial concerns.

Shantivanam
November 10, 1962

One does not enter into one's own self unless one enters into God, and one does not enter into God unless one enters into one's own self. It is the mystery of the Father and of the Son, totally other and nevertheless ineffably one, and the Spirit is their oneness. One does not become perceptible to one's self until one has perceived the depth of one's *I,* the *I* of the Son and the *Thou* of the Father. And the Spirit is this communication of the Father to the Son, of the Son to the Father, of me to God, of God to me, of Jesus to me, of me to Jesus. To be sure, the distinction must be strictly preserved. But read John 17. It is the very oneness of the Father and of the Son that is ours as a gift. I stated this rather strongly in the paper I sent last month, if you can decipher it. At rock bottom, is not all antinomy (in thought), all dilemma (in action) reducible to that: the Incomprehensible duality and non-duality, at one and the same time, of being, of God? The Son different from the Father, the Son one with the Father? Did not Jesus also feel this cleft? The temptation? The agony? Nevertheless it is only in the mystery of the cleft that the oneness is actualized. It is from the Father and from the Son, at once *one* and *two*, that the Spirit proceeds, the final Oneness of their consummation. One must enter into one's own self ever more deeply, but not in order to find the peace of escape. For the more one enters into one's own self, the more one penetrates the mystery of the Pleroma of the Lord and there one is never apart from one's brethren and from the Cross that spans the times. But the peace in this tension, the solution itself, without doubt, will not appear, neither on the plane of action nor on that of thought. But is not the purpose of all that which one thinks, of all that which one does, before all else, to make us realize in the profoundest depth this tension that is the Son, the "passage" *patrem,* that we realize (in Him) in time, this "leap out of one's own self" which is the essential feature of our faith? . . .

As I have already written you, I do not unfortunately master either my fatigue or my slumber. But slumber and fatigue, what does it matter: all is but sign, and the only work is the "descent" into "self," signified and realized by the movement of our thought and will. But this descent is so much truer than both! I believe that it would be necessary to work toward controlling the mental flow. I've read some American books that invite the reader to think of nothing at all for twenty minutes, for example, in the middle of the day. A sleep without the mind's invasion, vigilant as well against the invasion of dream, or better, reverie. Relaxation and non-effort. There is nothing more fatiguing (headache) than an Ignatian meditation and there is nothing more restful than the meditation of silence. In order to create this emptiness one must center oneself on an external or imaginary point, better still, on a movement of the body: the breath (a Buddhist teacher recommended that one center on the movement of the stomach provoked by breathing). Or, more simply, on the place of in-breath and out-breath. The field of consciousness is then "magnetized" and centered. Dissipation (which is the source of nervous tension) is transcended. Breathing then becomes rhythmic, the rhythm slows down and, little by little, the nervous system is becalmed. I think that that would be beneficial, at one and the same time, for prayer and work. Naturally this requires a first-rate effort of the will to "renounce all effort." The habit must be acquired slowly and steadily, one must agree to silence one's mind, to control its flow. The impassable and immobile "spectator" beyond the flow must be discerned. Then the flow no longer affects the psychological aspect of the entry into one's self. This must be practiced as an exercise from time to time. It procures a deepening of consciousness (better yet, of awareness)* attained from a more essential level of the consciousness of self, increasingly sheltered against the impact of outer excitations. The aim is not a renewed escape, but beyondness and transcendency. That must be experimented with in discretion, but I am persuaded that there is something there. What is essential is that this detachment be effected through relaxation. To force oneself, to struggle in the emptiness, would be a most dangerous form of tension.

LETTERS TO HIS FAMILY

> Arrival in India
> December morning
> August 15, 1948

I arrived here yesterday evening in the roadstead of Colombo. What joy, what emotion. As soon as I supped, it was 6:30 (2 o'clock back home), and I went up to the bow and began Vespers, the first Vespers of the Assumption of the Holy Virgin, my eyes fixed eastwards. The sun had already set and

---

*awareness in original text. Tr.

at the first psalm I saw a flash, the lighthouse of the port of Colombo, the first sign of marvelous India. Little by little lights flared alongside it, and the horizon soon scintillated with a myriad of lights, symbol of souls who wait and call. We dropped anchor in the port around eight o'clock. I felt nailed to the bulwarks, however, for someone tried to talk to me, and I replied with difficulty: here was an hour for which I had waited for fifteen years! The moon's crescent was reflected in the black water, the stars were few, the weather dark and dull.

The police came aboard, the formalities began. These Cingalese are consummately courteous. To simplify matters I have entrusted everything to the Cook Agency, thanks to which I'll be on the train at 7:30 this evening. I had slept on the boat and I got up very early, as you can imagine! Mass on board, the last, but it was already in my India which encompassed the port. Mass of the Assumption of Our Lady, her Entry into the heavens, my entry here, in thanksgiving and in offering. It is now 9 o'clock.

You will soon be getting up and thinking that I am here. I am about to disembark at once.

I am collecting my scraps of English, the Tamil language will be for tomorrow. And I am trying to get my bearings among the shillings, the rupees, the pounds.

So long.

I spent the morning in formalities at the office of the Cook Agency. Mysterious India is quite modern. It was a stroke of luck that I engaged the Agency and that we are five priests taking the train for Madras. I'll be in Kulitalai Tuesday afternoon.

Colombo has a grand look about it. I'll say more about it later. Unfortunately I didn't have any time to see anything.

From India much love.

Kulitalai
August 21, 1948

. . . No doubt you have already received my letter written last Sunday from Colombo. I am resuming my diary. Once I obtained my ticket and my luggage was checked . . . [illegible word] I was liberated from the solicitude—useful nevertheless—of the Cook Agency and I left to mail the letter. Everywhere there is pushing and elbowing and one doesn't know just how to break out of it. You can't take five steps without somebody offering you something. A certain Antonio followed me for a whole kilometer and waited for me stoically for a half hour. Looking for calm and peace, I ended up on an embankment on the edge of the beach and sat down on a bench. Immediately I was the center of attention of a constantly renewed crowd. For me this first contact with the Hindu throng was worth all the visits to the squares or buildings, which are very beautiful but too reminiscent of Europe. Conversations began, soon conducted by two Christians with whom I spoke, and not badly. After they left, a youngster who had been present from the start, trying to have a chat, came up to me. The conversation was on God, then on Christ, the Church. He was a boy of fifteen, whose parents were fervent Hindus, and who had been brought up in a Protestant secondary school. Visibly drawn to the Church, he had never been able to meet a Catholic priest until then. You should have seen him follow my English, no matter how badly pronounced, and avidly drink in everything I told him. Surely grace is seeking him! What a symbol on this day of arrival that this youngster should seek me out. It bowled me over. I didn't know any prayer in English, so I left with him my *Salve Regina* in Tamil which he read in front of me with great pleasure. I had to promise to write him. And I shall do so next week.

Dinner at the Hotel Métropole, 3 rupees, not bad. Then the

train. Cook was waiting for us, escorted us to our reserved coach. They have persuaded us to take couchettes which with our luggage would be much cheaper . . . essentially it was true. It would also be safer during the twenty four hour trip because the ordinary compartments were teeming with passengers. Crossed Ceylon by night and I saw nothing there, but after sleeping nine hours I woke up right in the terminal before the Tallimanar straits where the train moved along a lengthy stretch of woods. The ferry-boat waits on the other side, along with customs officials who were kind and obliging to us. Natives had to open all their packages and turn their pockets inside out, so the boat was around two hours late. As soon as we were settled the captain introduces himself and proposes to the Fathers that they say their Mass. We had not hoped for this and I was the only one who had fasted despite the solicitations of the sleeping-car steward. Everything necessary was on board, the altar was set up in the control room of the bridge. Served by a Tamil, the whole Tamil crew formed a circle, and genuflected. Communion served in India. You can imagine my emotion. A new smile from Providence. Mass on a Tamil boat, Tamil ambience. At first I had let the others speak in English with the Captain, later, alone with him, I expressed my joy . . . It was a two hour journey on the boat. I had forgotten the magnificent and symbolic sunset on that Colombo beach with the youngster. And on Monday morning the sunrise in T . . . on the East of the beyond, the one into which my companions from the *Champollion* are now sailing. Particulars given to the Indian police during the journey, then the arrival in India at D . . . at the end of a long strip of sand, poor and desert-like, with small children swimming around the boat crying out "*panam*" (money). The passengers would toss some pennies overboard and the children, in three or fours, would disappear under the water to gather the coins, clutching them between their teeth while waiting for another windfall. The Indian customs inspection is as long and as detailed as the

Cingalese; however, we were made to open our hand bags only as a matter of form and our big luggage was quickly passed on, luckily, for how would I ever have been able to open them or, rather, close them again? And towards noon the train took off, heading North. In Ceylon I had been in first class, compartments with two couchettes each with its own lavatory. Here, in second class, it was a compartment with a very large couchette on which one sat during the day and at night it accomodated two persons, one on top, the other below. It is really made for a long trip. India really gave me a poor welcome for my arrival. A long tongue of desert sand, then a reddish, uncultivated earth, more so than on Breton heathes, at times mini-jungles, some poorly cultivated fields, poor villages . . . At noon we went to the dining-car, and for 3 rupees (I think) I had a substantial repast. I had to go to India, travel in a couchette and sit in a dining car to practice ascesis! It was beneficial nevertheless because I arrived here in top form. We were four travelling North. You can imagine what barbs were teasingly directed at my enthusiasm by a missionary with a fifteen year background in India and who was there more out of duty than out of love for India . . . We were due to arrive in Trichy around 8 o'clock in the evening and go on our separate ways. Two were bound for Madras and beyond. Two were going west, to Bangalore, and me, I was staying on the train. As it was my turn to offer something, I suggested a brandy before we set out in different directions . . . we ordered it from the steward who at every station stop popped his head in to inquire about the needs of distinguished passengers, while the passengers, jam-packed in the other cars, were generously refreshed by a water-carrier at the doors. Unfortunately, we were in a dry district. For India has districts where all distilled, and even fermented, spirits are prohibited. I felt one with them when we clinked glasses containing lemon soda.

The train arrived ahead of time in Trichy. I get off with my luggage. Nobody at the station to meet the train, although I had wired. I took the underground passage and immediately ran into Father Monchanin with the emotion that you can imagine. I bid farewell to the others and set out for the bishopric. Under the cloister of the bishopric I meet the archbishop who accords me a welcome that is at once fatherly and hurried: supper, conversation, sleep. The bishopric is a vast, two-storied structure. Well-ventilated rooms, 3 by 6 meters at least, make up most of the building. Electric light. Tuesday morning Mass in the Cathedral, English-style breakfast, talk with the archbishop. I realize once more that I can talk with anyone who wants to talk with me. Then, I had to go to the police to introduce myself. We set out in an ox-cart. We are in the East, nobody is pressed for time, and moreover nobody really knows what my coming here is all about at the moment. We were sent from one office to another. That way we walked around in Trichy for two hours. Trichy is a big city with a population in the hundreds of thousands, I believe, of whom about twenty-thousand are Catholics. There are parishes, a big secondary school, several feminine religious institutes, but a truly Indian city, unlike Colombo. It is extremely extended and everywhere it is at once city and countryside. Contrasts: modern buildings and bamboo huts . . . We had no time to make visits. My luggage had been checked at Colombo for Kulitalai and it is better to have it come here directly. But we promised the archbishop to return next Monday.

Tuesday evening we took the train for Kulitalai. This time in third class with the crush. Kulitalai is 20 miles (35/40 km.) west of Trichy on the Erod line. I haven't yet told you about the Hindu crowds: perhaps I see them with my heart but I wouldn't be able to describe how likeable I find them. I did not find beauty in the Arabs of Algeria, nor in the Blacks of Djibouti. There is nothing marring about them as among yellow-complexioned peoples, for example, and you will often see beautiful jet-black hair. The complexion is very bronzed, but that seems quite natural. I seem to myself to have an abnormal complexion. They are much better clothed than I had imagined . . .

From Trichy to Kuli the countryside is pleasant and fertile, lined with coconut palms, palm trees, rice paddies. We are on the banks of the Kavery, a sacred river, of course, which brings fertility to the whole valley. The sun is setting. It's already dark when, one hour and a half later, we get off the train in Kulitalai. I pile my luggage on two *mattu vandi* and we head for the "rectory" which is very nearby. I arrive there at a marvelous hour, there's a full moon, the moon having just risen in the sky from which its diffused light gives the countryside a fairyland look. The *bhakti Ashram* (rectory) contains, in an enclosure, the church, quite simple in structure and ringed by coconut-palms, with the house behind it. The house, pure cubic style, is 15 meters in length and 4 in width, three rooms, windows on two sides, windows without panes with iron bars and shutters, a veranda in front. Next to it is another building which is the kitchen and the living quarters of the help. You can't imagine the beauty of a moonlight in the middle of coconut-palms. When I wake up at night, I go out to breathe in the air of the beauty.

So I have been here since Thursday evening, the 17th, in joy and peace. I'll tell you about it again later. If you only knew how everything here seems natural to me. It's as though I've been here since my childhood. The calm for prayer . . .

Here I am in a wholly Indian setting. Even the village is purely Indian. Nothing European mars it, save for some autos. It's a rather large market-town, the center for the surrounding countryside and which seems to me to be also a shopping center. There are shops at every step, with the merchant squatted in front of them. Children galore. One is not in Europe here. This is not a *black hole*. Next year I'll look for a more isolated spot, but already what calm!

My life here? I still have not had the right to a bare mat, mine is laid out on a wooden frame, and it will be necessary to change that next week. I also have a table and an arm-chair for the transitions must be negotiated slowly. But I eat India-style. You may be sure that there are not many rectories in India, whether or not the parish priest is Indian, in which one lives in the Indian way, except for here. Here one does not allow himself to place his hands or head in a wash-basin and thus wash himself in dirty water. On the sidewalk in front of the house is a copper wash-basin with a tumbler with which one does his ablutions by sprinkling water over himself. After a few days one notices that it is also convenient. At table a banana-leaf, almost rectangular, is placed in front of you—and this perhaps is less Indian—you fill it up with rice and then with a spoon you transfer it to a large plate. Then you compress it with your right hand and pour on it some sauce or *kolomb,* a sauce which varies constantly and which must be heavily spiced to be appreciated. You knead the whole with your right hand, previously passed under the water and you bring the rice to your mouth with your fingers. After the first plate you begin again with a sauce made of *tayir,* a kind of tart curdled milk. Squeeze a half-lemon on it and it's delicious. With that come large glasses of water poured by your "cook," a banana to top off the meal and, of course, the final washing of the right hand. What else is needful for happiness? In the morning *cafe au lait* and local pastry. Is this not luxury for one who comes here to practice ascesis? I forgot to mention that one uses the right hand only when eating, the other being reserved for usages of a "lower" order.

There are no pews or chairs in the church; one kneels or one sits down India-style. I am so happy to be part of praying India. Attendance at Mass is relatively higher than back home. And the Indian greeting! No brutal handshakes as in Europe, but the gracious gesture of folded palms raised to the level of the chin. And Christians bow or kneel before their *sami* (priest) upon extending this greeting. In return I must give them the *"arsivadam,"* that is to say, I pronounce what signifies a blessing by raising my right hand, if not making the sign of the cross on their foreheads. Because I still cannot talk to them in Tamil.

Little by little I'll be giving you further details on this interesting life. The correspondence of view and thought between me and Father M . . . is extraordinary. A providential encounter. The sense of the work to be undertaken is taking shape with utter naturalness. I'll discuss it again later. Without further delay I should like to give you a glimpse of my life here. The heat is not so terrible. It was worse on the boat. I limit my underclothing to the extreme, in the *ashram* we even walk around without sandals which we wear only for Mass and trips to town. In the bishopric the archbishop himself is bare foot in sandals which he takes off in his room. Here everybody goes bare foot. I sleep a lot, even in the afternoon, in short, in order to lead the life of an ascetic! I am waiting to habituate myself to the local customs, as prudence requires, especially since I have an arduous intellectual work to produce. Don't be vexed with me if I tell you of my happiness here because I know at what price you and I have purchased it. But is not my happiness also yours? I have not yet received any news from home. How eagerly I await it! My letter will arrive too late for the feast of St. Louis which I would have thought about nevertheless together with all your anniversaries of this month. I'll write again next week. My time is four hours and a half ahead of French summer time. You are just about having dinner, and I'm going to have some tea. With much, much love to all.

Henri

June 21, 1958

. . . It's already ten years since I left Kergonan, Saint-Briac and France. To be sure I regret nothing. May the Lord be blessed for all that which He gives me here. I don't understand the missionaries of long ago who constantly preserved a nostalgia for their homelands! I was talking about this only a few days ago with a monk who came to see me. It would be like a wife with her husband and children missing her birthplace. Nothing could ever re-pay for that which India gives to anyone if one gives oneself with his or her whole heart. It's rare, perhaps! So much the worse for those who do not know how to understand her.

. . . Peace and joy to all, as St. Paul said when he wrote his letters. When one knows that God is, that He dwells within our hearts, beyond all the contingencies, when one no longer considers the Good Lord as someone to whom one prays in order to receive this or that, but whom one loves, whom one adores for Himself because He is, because He is love . . . then joy and peace spread along the whole line and soon the furrowed brow is smoothed.

Much love to all.

Henri

August 25, 1958

. . . External conditions are of no matter. There is a pearl to be found by each one in the depth of his or her heart. And if one finds it, what matters if one is bed-ridden and poor! We are, as long as we are, drawn by what is external to us, we pray to obtain health, money, reputation . . . One might even say that the Good Lord has been made for that! But true religion is to love Him, to adore Him at all times and in all places, independently of any reward to us. And He puts us to the test in order to teach us that, in order to make us understand that there is one essential consideration—God. He who is Love in himself, He who is to be adored, He in whom one forgets and one loses oneself. We do everything we can. And then after that we surrender ourselves to His discretion. We reason that He is. And then that is all. This is the secret of happiness.

If only I could make you understand it. Do you think that without that I would be so happy in my solitude when nothing that I dreamed of as a development of Shantivanam has turned out, after I found myself completely alone last year and everybody was saying (and wishing) that Shantivanam was finally about to be closed down . . . If only I could make you understand all that . . .

LETTERS TO FATHER LEMARIÉ[1]

Shembaganur
March 4, 1955

. . . This morning I climbed to the top of Arunachâla (a 2-hour hike). Mid-way I was lost in the clouds. From the height, the wind at times swept away the fog and made a corner of the horizon appear as in a mirage. "From the summit of Arunachâla, how could the world still exist?"

In Arunachâla I often take part in a *Bhavan* (religious chant) after having for a long time declined to do so. And now I had to sing in my turn after having declared myself incompetent. The *Salve,* the paschal *Gloria,* the *Agios o Theos, Veni sancte, alleluia, introit* of midnight with commentary: the call of the Spirit and then the mystery of the birth within. My hosts are very appreciative and I must sing at every reception. One time we had a kind of pentecostal glossolalia. One chanted in Sanskrit, Tamil, Hindi, Gujarati, Bengali, an English lady in English and German. I chimed in with pericopes from the *Gloria, Agios o Theos* and *Alleluia,* and the French canticle of Lourdes (the only French canticle I know that could match the inspiration and the charm of that which the others were chanting).

Shantivanam
March 28, 1955

. . . But when Father Monchanini returns from his latest journey to Pondi (Pondi for him is what Arunachâla is for me), I'll tell him frankly that I have decidedly given up his idea in regard to intellectuals. What I want are Christian *sannyasis,* intelligent ones, to be sure, but not intellectuals. The intellectual temptation is as dangerous for the monk as is the temptation of work, industrial or liturgical . . .

Shantivanam
May 16, 1955

. . . Be bold! And from the "Manifested" plunge into the "non-manifested" and the "non-manifestable" and lose yourself in them.

Elephanta
July 1, 1955

. . . On Friday I saw an extraordinary Buddhist monastery north of Bombay, Kaukeri (12th century), 109 caves cut in the rock, a temple also rock-cut, a chapter-house. Beautiful sculptures of Buddha, of an unimaginable serenity. In the jungle on the side of a hill the sea is visible on the horizon, about 5 miles (u km.) from the highway. It made an extraordinary impression on Father M. and on me. How we would like to repopulate all that. Last night we came here to Elephanta. Here Hindu temples are carved in the rock, only one of which is well preserved. *Staggering* for me. I am more

Hindu than Buddhist. You know the three-headed Siva incorrectly called Trimurti, at least by our post-marks. No image can give an idea of it. When I glimpsed it, I had to lean against a column for support: what serenity and what concentration in Siva the creator, the central figure! I remained late for a long time yesterday evening contemplating it and let its influence soak into me in the darkness that ensued. This morning we said our Mass directly opposite it.

. . . How all that is marvelously detaching: just as physical fatigue at times liberates one from the vagrancies of the mind, the dashing of one's hopes marvelously liberates one from the superficial self and aids one to penetrate to the mystery of the true self, to the pith and marrow of the depth, of the *guha* . . .

Shantivanam
December 24, 1955

Father Monchanin doesn't want to see the problem, his soul is unruffled and he accuses me of being discouraged, unstable and sporadic in my fervor . . . He forgets that if he himself had agreed to work at making Shantivanam a reality while there was still time, things perhaps might have taken a different course. Discouraged by his inertia, I have been saved by Arunachâla and from now on I can no longer escape there . . .

Wednesday
March 14, 1956

Dear Father,

Your letter arrived just in time yesterday evening to remind me that the feast of St. Joseph was near . . . It is not that I don't often think of you and of all those experiences that I would like to communicate to you by word of mouth. But here, the time! the place? I have just lived through 2/3 weeks among the most unforgettable ones of my sojourn in India. This time in a complete hindu, brahmianical, sivaist setting, not only alongside them, but living with them like one of them . . .

I had an appointment with my guru, Sri Gnana-Aranda (wisdom-beatitude), on the second Sunday of Lent. When I arrived he was absent. So I was received by the brahmin of the neighboring village. I was lodged in the Temple where they would bring my food. Alone at night with the lingam, the sacred symbol of Siva. I'll try to describe all this to you in a few pages which I'll be sending you soon. It was then that I understood the mystery hidden in Hinduism in the sivaist cult.

I've been here for 15 days with my guru. I have been totally "captivated." The petty details of everyday living have not been able to change my first impression. One prostrates oneself before him with a veneration that suffuses the whole soul and at his feet one feels enveloped by a fatherly tenderness and, in turn, one is animated by the tenderness and the trust of a child towards him . . . Were this man to ask me to leave tomorrow and walk naked and mute along the roads like Sada Siva Brahman, I could not refuse him. The mysterious ways of Providence. This encounter completed, and on to a higher plane, that with my Parsee in Bombay! What will become of all that? In him, I felt the truth of the *advaita* . . . He would like that henceforth I devote all my time to a meditation without thought, setting aside not only all distraction but also useless conversation and even all reading. He assures me that the experience will come soon if I act thus and I am [a missing word]. But he has understood that I cannot suddenly break off from Shantivanam. But less than ever before will my heart be in Shantivanam. Here complete silence reigns, save for him. It's the only way to avoid importunate questions. And he knew that I was grateful for this and defended me, he who never wanted to talk of his past. Is there, moreover, a past for a true *jnani*? Of the self he says: not only must one not tell others of what it was, but the very remembrance of it must disappear from one's own heart . . .

The pull, greater than ever, of this advaitin abyss, the abyss of Arunachâla . . . What a shock when one has intensely lived the Christian *sacrament*. Here one "wrests" the sign from you. No reading, no prayer no *puja* (Mass for us, external worship entirely)—only and continually *dhyana:* this meditation without thought for those who are capable of it. No Mass here, naturally, and the breviary is recited altogether *privatim* in an hour each midday. Once the *res* is obtained, the sacrament recaptures all its meaning, but when one finds himself in the uncircumscribed space between the sign and the *res,* drawn irresistibly by the one and not feeling that one has the right to abandon the other . . .

The other Sunday was a "night of Siva" and chants were the rule: it is not like these pseudo-vigils of Christmas or Easter in which one gets up for two hours in the middle of the night. Chants, dances around the sacred flame. Hinduism has an extraordinary sense of the play of God in creation. Christianity is tragic, it takes the creation wholly seriously; the Hindu knows that the creation does not exhaust God. The *advaitin* can be a sivaist and play his role in this mirage-world. Can he be a Christian? Christianity, perhaps, is too perfect. It has so admirably absorbed God into itself that it is very difficult to find "God in one's self" again in it.

How far I am here from SHV and from its future, from articles etc. Would I still be able to "play" the "role" of writing about the ideal of SHV? I would require months, perhaps years of great silence to take stock in regard to this point which transcends the intelligence. And how make the Greeks, who are the Christians, understand that God and Intelligence essentially have nothing in common with all that which we can conceive of mind and of intelligence on the human, or especially the angelic, mode. You can divine the deep shock of these two weeks. I'll try to write about them for a very restricted circle that can understand it. But now it is the deep immersion beyond the sign . . . The incomprehensible ways of Providence. I now know what a guru is and what a *jnani* is (two identical things for that matter); it is from these *jnanis* and gurus that India has lived. I'll write you again after Easter. Excuse me for talking to you only about this mystery "felt" here. Father X. returned just before I left; next week I'll discuss the future with him.

Happy feast-day. Chant Easter under the signs, you who can still do so . . .

Arunachâla
Thursday, March, 1956

. . . My guru would like to prescribe a time free of all—of all reading, of all meditation on the object. I feel that it is in the offing.

I re-said the Mass this morning in the room of the Trappist, Hindu, Sufi ex-novice, now a fervent disciple of Gnananda. I act as interpreter for him when he comes to see the Teacher (Tirukovilur which is 30 km. south-east of Tiruvanna). From the ashram one can see the holy mountain . . .

Holy Wednesday
March 28, 1956

. . . Very frank conversation with Father X. If he remains in SHV he conceives it as a laura in which each lives in silence (excellent) and in which one of the hermits will *sacrifice* himself (he is quite ready) to form the possible aspirants, absolutely as he pleases with no control or possible consultation with the others who at most, at the very most, will be called

on to give a class of chant or to lend a hand with manual
work. This is very utopian, of course, and not viable, but it
shows quite clearly that no *efficacious collaboration* is en-
visageable. I much prefer that he orient himself on Malabar.
Father Monchanin is beginning to realize the gravity of the
situation . . . I incline increasingly towards a separate hermitage, and if one day the Lord should send some disciple I
will try to help him become quite simply a *sannyasi*

Trivandrum
September 18, 1956

Dear Father,
. . . Is it a dream with no tomorrow that I am confiding to
you today! and will I soon again be seized by the staggering
call of the Hindu abyss of Arunachâla? What do you think of
all that?
Why do you deplore not being able to penetrate this abyss?
To be sure one can penetrate it only in a naked way, horribly
naked, but also what a call! It is not a question of hurling
oneself in it, but simply one of not resisting the engulfment,
the mystery of interiority.

Shantivanam
October 13, 1961[1]

. . . Father Monchanin does not have his "plan" in his
head; he lets things proceed as they are. But, in fact, no collaboration with him is possible since collaboration presupposes "plan"; despite all his amiability, his gentleness, his
erudition, his virtue and his "fervor"! He is the best of companions, but the worst of "partners" (of which he is not
aware). So it's best to take his side, leave him to guard SHV
and let the work start elsewhere. He will surely not like the
idea, but if Father X does not go to Trivandrum, my present

intention is to go there myself. I no longer prize SHV, I think it's about time that I go out and work for the Church elsewhere, otherwise I don't know whether I'll be able to resist for long the call, so irresistible, of authentic *sannyasa*. The greatest difficulty is the case of Father X. It is very clear that he holds on to me above all, he soon guessed the real situation. I prefer, of course, that he work apart from me (we are 4 priests each one of us too richly endowed as personalities and too independent), but he needs me for an x period of time . . . It would be necessary to shuttle back and forth for a spell.

Shantivanam
October 31, 1956

. . . And there is hardly any solution. I believe that there is only one real solution to our anguish: to go beyond the concept, to this mystery of the depth which, however, shines forth only for those who have dared to penetrate it by drastically going beyond the whole level of sense and intelligence, namely the experience to which the *advaita* of our *rishis* invites us. Alas, I myself have not yet dared to place myself in the conditions of this experience . . . Nevertheless even its dawn is beatifying and gives joy of life regardless of the nature of the surface tides.

Shantivanam
December 11, 1936

. . . There is perhaps a duty to reveal to the Church these riches that India has in reserve for her! For all that is quite new, I believe . . . or rather I fear!
. . . Nevertheless what profound manifestations of goodness have been revealed to me—Arunachâla, etc. And how the Christian would like to find the Father again at the

profound depth of this *Atman,* of this *brahman*! But the theologians have so imprisoned—if I dare say so—the truth of the Father and of the Son and of the Spirit, like the spider who spins a kind of cocoon around its victim, so that one is hard put to find in it the mystery of the whole of Arunachâla . . .

Silane
July 14, 1959

Dear Father,

I was hoping to find a word from you here before writing you for the 25th. But it's best to write you immediately. For it will be difficult once I resume my peregrinations. I have just returned from a marvelous journey to the sub-Himalayan regions, always on the move, on foot (120 km.), in a bus etc. It was most marvelous on foot, clambering up hills, skirting valleys . . . solitudes, silence. I was stopped on the bridge of Karna-Prayag since my permit had not arrived in time. However the permit did arrive here (near Simla) and I'll go in August, or if possible in September (after the rains) to the places of the great interior pilgrimages of the Himalayas. I went down the Ganges again in the mountain as far as Rishikesh, Hardwar. The mountain slopes downward, diverges, the Ganges spills onto the plain, the Shakti, the Mother. An impression of grandeur, of sacredness. In Rishikesh, a large town of monks, somehow a disappointment . .. 10 kilometers, all along the Ganges, of ashrams, huts, laure . . . monks of all shades in all kinds of dress and non-dress walk about . . . in the evening they sit on the bank in meditation . . . A non-stop pilgrimage, an Indian Lourdes. All the pilgrims of the mountain pass through there and take their first bath there; every day buses bring 1000 to 1500 pilgrims upstream and they still have 120 km., 300 km., some 500 km. to go on foot in order to complete their pilgrimage. The Ganges flows rapidly here, like a mountain stream, the crowd presses forward to bathe in its waters. In the evening the *puja** on the river. Tiny boats made of leaves filled with flowers, with a tiny lamp that flickers out, are floated on the river . . . a deep impression . . . The Himalayas have captivated me, whether it be the inward solitudes, or the mouths of the Ganges towards which the monks veneratingly make haste.

. . . The Spirit who "broods" on the water also hovers over the Ganges. To us, the descendants of the *rishis,* it is our Jordan. When the Christian bathes in it, is it not in the name of Jesus coming to John, the *rishi* and the prophet, the *diksha*[1] of the *sannyasa*! In Rishikesh, I was able to say the Mass of the Visitation. *Ut audivit salutationem Mariae Elizabeth* . . . As soon as Elizabeth heard Mary's greeting . . . the infant that India bears in her womb. When will the greeting of the Church to India be sufficiently effulgent so that the infant may exult?

Shantivanam
July 18, 1966

. . . I must have also told you of the very interesting letters I received, in regard to my books, coming from cloistered or secular contemplatives. They can be summarized as follows: your book has taught me nothing truly new. But for the first time I recognized the path along which God had been leading me for a long time! Proof that the *advaitine* dimension of the contemplative prayer is not a sectarian Hindu datum, but a value of a universal order—hence catholic—which simply has been set in bolder and purer relief in the upanishadic tradition . . .

---

*A petitional prayer recited before a god's image. Tr.

Gyansu
June 15, 1970

Very Dear Father, Brother,

Upon returning from Montserrat you must have found my news from Indore, I believe. I too have just returned. Dog-tired, but enriched. An encounter above all with young people from France, Switzerland, Belgium, university student protesters, but what first-rate boys and girls. How I feel *at home** and in deep rapport with them.

. . . It seems that at the present time there is a grave crisis among the rites in Kerala. An Indian rite would be necessary to resolve it. But *a rite is not invented.* It "springs up" from the depth of the soul. Moreover, attachment to the rite is above all a quest for identity and fear of losing one's little "I."

What are the monasteries of France waiting for in order to respond to the spiritual call of these young people who come here in quest of the inner life. Are those who discover the best of India those who have visited a Trappist or Carthusiam monastery in which true monks live a true inner life? The crisis is first of all of an interior order. And the remedy is beyond forms. The return to the well-spring of Monasticism. Beyond the Liturgy itself. That seems to me to be the most urgent task . . . And that must be given in the mental schemes of the West. Indian mental schemes disconcert anyone who has not penetrated the *inmost* self. The hippies, of course, are another matter. They are in Nepal and in Gore and for the moment the Indian police have their hands full with them.

Poona
Thursday, April, 1972

. . . Every day contemplative reading of the *Upanishads* with discreet Christian overtones, meditation of pure silence,

---

*In English in original. Tr.

Mass in free rhythm in connection with upanishadic texts. Very interesting and well received. These young people will climb on our shoulders and reach the pinnacle.

July 17, 1973

At some time or other you must have certainly enjoyed the words of Silesius: "What matters it to me if Christ is dead and risen as long as it is not a truth for me?" India liberates from the past as well as from the future . . . There is nothing else but the eternal instant in which I am. This name of I AM which Jesus applies to himself in John is for me the key to his mystery. And it is the discovery of this Name in the depth of one's own "I AM" which truly constitutes salvation for each one . . .

. . . So you see, for us here, Europe, the Church, even the best, seem to live only on the surface of their being the "mystery" of the Spirit who murmurs in Paulinian terms thou art "son of God," or in our terms here "thou art that." People squabble over the ministry, over celibacy, and the rest, and one forgets that one thing only matters, to awaken.

Indore
September 22, 1973

Dear Father and Brother,

Today I received your letter of August 28. In the meanwhile you must have received the account that I sent you of my "adventure" in the bazar of Rishikesh (July 14). I suffered a heart attack as I was about to take the bus—but one which providential circumstances are keeping within curable limits. At the same time a marvelous experience of "crossing" between life and death, the discovery that one IS! What do the situations matter? Joy and serenity which made unforgettable the two weeks that I spent motionless in bed. I spent 2 weeks in Rishikesh, then 3 in Rapjur (Dehra Dun) and as soon as possible I came to Indore . . . This morning's cardiogram was better than last month's; however, it is not yet normal. I'll probably spend the winter as a guest in a Carmelite monastery. Even recovered, my life of wild independence is finished. I'll no longer have the strength to live by myself nor to clamber up the cliffs of the bank of the Ganges in Uttarkashi. Where will I alight next year? *Dominus providebit.* But I see nothing clearly, for I cannot live alone.

Indore
December 3, 1973

Dear Father and Brother,

Since Advent began yesterday—*in illa die* this enchantment of the future which rejoins the *in illo tempore*—is enchantment of the past . . . whereas here everything brings us back towards the HIC and NUNC, *kai nun.* Therefore since Advent has begun, Merry Christmas and Happy New Year! I am not yet in shape to write you at length. Since July I have been incapable of any concentrated attention. At any rate it's a marvelous lesson not to seek the truth in literature and in flowery language. I have done that all too much. At the end of October I was in a tight corner or, rather, the body seemed to be crying for mercy and I had really lost all taste to *survive.* Now, barring the accident of a relapse—frequent shortness of breath—it has revived and seems to be on the upswing. But it will require many months before a minimum of physical and psychic forces is recovered. It's up to God! In all things thanks be to God for descents and ascents alike . . .

This morning I must take the plane to go to Madras, towards the *Sun,* but our Air-Inter (Indian Airlines) has been on strike—a lockout—for the past two weeks. I can't travel by train unaccompanied, above all because of the transfers. And I have no one here to take along with me. By the time I call someone and reserve my tickets there's a good chance that the planes will be flying again. Finally there is, there will be, a touch of irony about this state of affairs. On two occasions this year I refused to take the plane to participate in the Seminars in Bangalore, and now I am practically forced to fly for reasons of survival. The cold is beginning to get harsh in the North and it will be very bad for me to remain confined in a room by the fireside or rather in front of an electric radiator.

Note: Father Le Saux never had to take the plane for southern India. He died on the evening of December 7, following pulmonary complications.

LETTER TO FATHER MIQUEL[1]

Shantivanam
June 19, 1956

Dear Father,
    . . . A "Greek" must pass through the dark night of the Cross in order to accept the absolute "intellectual" divestment that India has the mission to demand from the world and, above all, from the Christian world. God is *neti, neti* . . . Any "idea" of Him is an "idol." The man who is the most Greek Christian, less than others perhaps, cannot accept giving up the satisfaction of having abandoned himself to God, of knowing *himself* to be God, of loving himself as God. India, in a twinkling, throws you into that dark night. In the West one utters loud cries. It's a torture, says John of the Cross. But to us here that seems so natural.

The theological problems that this fundamental intuition poses and this fire that, immediately upon being kindled, consumes all that which the intellect can produce, are certainly very grave. And I am far from having resolved them. Nevertheless they must be faced. They are the very instrument of this necessary incessant purification of the "formalism" that constantly threatens the Church—a divine mystery—by reason of her insertion in *thought*, in *cult* and in *social organism* . . .

Normally all that is the work of monks, for it is the monk who has the ecclesial mission of penetrating the depths of Being, as we would say here, much less as a theologian (which is only a first step) than as a *seer,* if seeing can still express itself in words. And that is the profound reason for being of Shantivanam, to lead the Christians of India to release in the depth of their Hindu soul the message which "mysteriously" springs up from there and upon releasing it to transmit it to the Church and to the world.

PART THREE

Unpublished Excerpts from the Journal

of Henri Le Saux

Swami Abhishiktananda

1952-1973

1952: July 24

The sage is he who takes refuge in the center of his own self, leaving his intellect and his body outside . . . where one discovers oneself as *absolute;* where, in truth, one encounters *God in the form of Self.* God "purified" of all the imaginative and conceptual raiments in which He has been attired from the outset. God in the distinctness and nakedness of His Absolute . . . not that there one feels that he is facing God, not that there one feels oneself to be God . . . All conceptualization will be subsequent and will bear the mark of mental, ethical, hereditary and acquired categories. One simply *IS.* And this fundamental experience is at one and the same time that of unique and simple Existence.

September 14

Lord Jesus has expressed his special relationship to God in the terms Father-Son, which He found in the Jewish tradition, by giving the relationship a new meaning. This ever more marvellous, ever more total awakening of the human consciouness of Christ and his divine Consciousness.

1953: September 27

I have tasted all too much of the *advaita* for me to be able henceforth to regain the "gregorian" peace of a Christian monk. I have tasted all too much, formerly, of this "gregorian" peace not to be anguished in the depth of my *advaita*.

1956: February 9

Man has constantly oscillated, and will always oscillate, between these two poles of the apprehension of the Absolute: the Other and the Me of me, Self of self. There is no (nondualist) *advaitin* who one day or other will not say THOU to God; and there is no sociological religion, dualist as it may be, in which one or the other of its adepts will not cry out like Al Hallaj: "Remove this Thou who is between Thee and me."

November 9

Beginning of the long retreat in silence in Mauna Mandir Kumbakonam (November 6-December 8)
Meditation on being is at best nothing else but meditation on the Presence. And thus "our" Yoga could be presented to the Christian. To immerse oneself in the Presence. To create the silence of the imagination, of thought, the silence even of the idea of Presence. And then the flashing Presence. The Presence is being, Shekinah, the Presence is Glory.
Enter in joy. Enter into the Presence. Enter in being. The paradox of the created condition: to attain being! As though being could be attained? Who then attains it if it is not being that he attains? And yet if being is, how would it be able to attain to being?

There is no longer anything else then than Presence . . . The Presence is the name of Being so long as the veil has not yet been rent . . . In the Presence I am finally present to myself. Who is present: The One Who is *PRESENT*. The awakening to Presence.

Christ present to Self in the bosom of the Father, in the essential Presence of the Father. To live in the present is to live in the Presence. In being . . . The continued awakening of Jesus to the Presence, from the initiation of his consciousness in Mary's womb up to the eternal awakening in the dawn of Easter, the Passage.

November 14

I have come here (to India) to make you known to my Hindu brothers, and it is Thou (Jesus) who has made Thyself known to me here through their mediation, in the staggering lineaments of Arunachâla!

November 16

The Trinity is the interpretation by the Greek mind of the impact on the Jews and on the Helleno-Christians of the experience of Jesus in his Depth.

1958: June 10

How awaken in Hindu souls this experience of Christ which is the aim of all Christian preaching, and not simply a mental and practical conformity to an outward norm, as is most frequently the case. This experience of Christ is the Spirit suddenly swooping down on the believer as recounted in the Acts. It is the deep conviction through shock in the inmost recess of being that Christ is there, living and present, that His life and my life are an indivisible, twinned system of stars, that He is in the inmost recess of my life and I am in the inmost recess of His.

1963: August 20

The Christian is the one to whom Jesus has "communicated" his experience of being of the Father, and of going to the Father: *processio et transitus,* that which constitutes him person.

1966: December 21

The baptism of Jesus was for him the fundamental experience on which his whole life depended. He had the experience of being possessed by the Spirit of God, this Spirit of Yahweh that the Old Testament had announced (Isaiah 11, 2). "On him the spirit of Yahweh rests." He had the experience in the same time of being the Son of God and the experience of God the Father.

The baptism gives nothing to Jesus, yet it reveals to him who He is.

1970: October 3

If Ramada had lived in a Christian milieu he would have been a saint in the same manner of the others, but of a different experience. And if Jesus had been born in an *advaitin* milieu, would not the expression of his experience have been wholly different?

1971: July 2

This I AM, this awakening to me, it is the very awakening of God to self . . .

July 24

Whether I wish it or not, I am profoundly attached to
Christ Jesus and therefore to the ecclesial *koinonia*. It is in
him that the "mystery" disclosed itself in me, since my
awakening to my own self and to the world. It is in his image,
his symbol that I know God, and that I know my own self
and the world of men. Since my awakening to new depths
within me of self*, this symbol has undergone a marvelous
amplification. Christian theology had already disclosed to me
the eternity of the mystery of Jesus in *sinu Patris*. Later India
revealed to me the cosmic whole of this mystery—this revelation, in which the Judaean revelation inserts itself.

But for me Jesus is my Sadguru. It is in him that God appeared to me, it is in his *mirror* that I recognized myself, by
adoring him, by loving him, by consecrating myself to Him.

1972: August 25

Abba, the mystery of non-distance!
And it is to this "non-distance" with the Lord, with the
one who is called God, that Jesus invites us.
India has been so fascinated by this non-distance that she
has named it non-duality, and even *ekatvam* (oneness).
For how can one distinguish anything whatsoever, anyone
whomsoever, in a divine non-distance? And it is this non-
distance that Jesus reveals among men, re-veals: unveils,
shows and also realizes—sign of the very communion of
bread.
How Jesus must have enjoyed his earthly family, Mary and
Joseph so that, spontaneously, he signified his great experience in the word *Abba*.

———————

*self in original. Tr.

1973: April 19

As long as I consider the Trinity apart from me, i.e., me the subject who beholds, who considers "that," *"tad,"* the Trinity, the object that is considered by me, to be pure dvaitam (duality), it is speculation and abstraction. If I am only in an outward relationship with the Trinity, the Trinity has no meaning for me. It has meaning for me only when the *antariksha,* the firmament that exists between it and me shatters and I can contemplate it from within, from the very eye with which God sees Himself. The Son knows the Father—but according to John and Paul, I myself am son . . . and I know the Father in the *Abba* that I pronounce. And I know the Son in the *I* (that I am) who pronounces Abba.

1973: September 11

It is clear from my remembrances, from my conversations at that time (after July 14) and from the letters written then, that I first experienced the cardiac crisis as a marvelous spritual adventure. The center of the intuition that forced itself on me in these first days was that the awakening is independent of any situation whatsoever, of all the *dvandvas,* and first of all of the *dvandva* called life-death. One awakens everywhere and simply, and the awakening cannot be confused with that which one sees at the moment of the awakening and therefore with that through which one becomes conscious that one is awakening.

The first night was filled with difficult dreams, not nightmares however. I was made to pass from cave to cave, at different altitudes, 9,000, 11,000, 13,000 feet. The snows of Kashmir mingled with the banks of the Ganges. And I constantly replied: the awakening has nothing to do with "measuring oneself" against ever more difficult living conditions. It occurs no matter what the circumstance. *I awaken* at any instant of life, in any actual circumstance. There was also in these nights a sharp sense of the smallness of the body, from heaad to toe. The difficulty of persuading oneself that this minimum of matter should suffice to support consciousness.

At the end of a few days the marvelous solution of an equation came to me: I have discovered the GRAIL. And I say and I write that to anyone who can grasp the image. At bottom the quest for the Grail is nothing else but the quest for Self. A unique quest signified in all the myths and symbols. It is one's own self that one is seeking through all. And in this quest one runs in every direction, whereas the Grail is here, nearby, one has only to open one's eyes. And it is the discovery of the Grail in its last truth, Galahad's direct look inside the vessel instead of being merely nourished by the Grail, nor even drinking from the Grail, which mysteriously traverses the hall.

In these weeks of grace, I had the very distinct impression that it was a "renewal" of life that had been given to me, something beyond the measure assigned to me by "life," and that I did not have the right to misuse it. This grace of awakening—return to life—is not for me but for others. It was so clear: it was to proclaim the discovery of the Grail, to say to the world: *Uttistha, purisha,* Awake, arise Parusha! (Katha Upanishad 3, 14), discover the Grail. Behold, it is in the depth of thee, it is this very I that thou pronouncest in each instant of thy conscious life, even in the depth of thy consciousness as dreamer, as sleeper. A life that is henceforth in the service of this Awakening. The manner thereof? Of that I can know nothing. But it was very clear to me that here, for me, there is a fundamental cleft in my life.

At the end of several weeks the routine resumed naturally, but the vista disclosed by these days of grace is always a Light that illumines within.

It is the final touch of the intuition that marked me in January: "All has become clear." There is only the AWAKENING. All that which is "notion," myths and concepts is but the expression of it. There is neither sky, nor earth, there is only Purusha who I am . . .

I had the impression, so distinct, of a struggle in me between the angel of death and the angel of life. This "death thrust" had been looking for me for a long time. In the last years I have often said that I live under the sign of *Mritya* (Death), but it was quite different from that which happened in June-July.

. . . And nevertheless, without my feeling it, there it was: the angel of life, the life thrust that fought against the death thrust. The circumstances, so manifestly providential, that accompanied my attack. Something in me that fought so that I *should survive* the encounter with that which was struggling in me to bear me away.

FOOTNOTES

CHAPTER 1

1. Published in the Proceedings of the Congress of Bangalore, 1973.
2. "I am the Lord and there is no other."
3. Is: Being, Atman, the Self, the inmost principle of man, the supreme self, Brahmani: the supreme principle of all, the absolute *Eikam eva advitiyam:* unique and without peer.
4. Congress of Bangalore, 1973.

CHAPTER 2

1. Unpublished, 1971.

CHAPTER 3

1. Unpublished, 1971.

SECTION II

1. *Purusha,* the Person, the archetypal man of the sacrifice from whom came the origin of the world: total man in his plenitude of being. The Spirit, The One who dwells in the heart of man.
2. *Sat-Guru:* the true spiritual Teacher, the one who initiates to consciousness through the personal experience that he himself has of God.
3. *Bhakti:* Devotion, the way of devotional love.

SECTION III

1. Powers who preside over the cosmic order, personalized manifestations of the divine Power at work in the universe.

CHAPTER 4

1. Written in 1964, published in *Carmel,* 7963/I, 1965 II.
2. *A-dvaita:* non-duality; *a-dvitya:* not-two; *advaitin:* the one who has "realized" the non-duality of being or, at least, who believes in it on the strength of his teachers and of the Scriptures.
3. As the Katha-Upanishad (4/1) says: "The senses of man are outward/going, hence he looks outwardly and not inwardly into the interior mystery: the one or the other, however, who is wise, desirous of immortality returns his eyes to within and beholds the Self!"
4. See previous footnote.
5. *Lila:* game, the "game" of the Lord in the creation.

6. *Karma:* work, action, from which: service (*seva*). In the old days the *karma* was considered more as the enjoined observance of the ritual acts, somewhat akin to the Jewish Torah, encompassing all life and finding florescence in the cult of the Temple.

7. *Bhakti:* devotion, piety; the *bhakta* is the one who approaches God principally through this way.

8. *Vedanta:* (veda-anta: the end of *Veda*, the last or philosophic part of the Hindu Scriptures (or *Veda*) = the Upanishads. The philosophic doctrine that expounds the *advaitin* intuition, center of the upanishadic revelation, is also called *vedanta.*

9. *Sannyasi:* the "renouncing one" or Hindu monk, also called *sadhou* (the "boh", the "virtuous one"—*sannyasa:* the state of the "renouncing one").

10. *Guha:* cave, mystically that "cavern of the heart", the deepest center of the soul, there where dwells the Lord, more exactly where the last mystery of the soul and of God ineffably is revealed. *A-dvaita,* non-dual (note that the *advaita* is not reducible either to monism or pantheism despite simplifications of it that are often given.

11. A monastery of the Eastern Church in which a community of monks lived communally, but in separate cells. Tr.

12. *Devas,* the *dii* (gods) of the Latin tradition; dwellers in the abode of light (*dyu*). They are also the cosmic "forces" at work in the universe and in the "elements", and the "powers" who rule our senses and our faculties. The upanashadic revelation insists on their non-identification with the Absolute (Brahman or Atman) and on the necessity to go beyond them in order to arrive at the "realization."

13. *Atman:* the last principle of being, its "deepest center", the essence, the spark of the soul, the "Self", this entity in which one is *self* independently of any outer conditioning, mental or sensorial.

14. Brahman: the ultimate principle, the "foundation" and the "depth" of all that which exists, the *Absolute,* beyond all that which can be grasped or thought by man, even by the *devas.* The supreme revelation of the Upanishads is that the *atman* is *brahman.* But this can be realized only in an *intuition* or in an *experience* that infinitely goes beyond conceptual thought and that comes to one in the waiting in the depth of the *guha,* in the profoundest depth of self (*atman*) and in the profound depth of the supreme mystery (*brahman*), at one and the same time (*a-dvaita*).

15. *Pranava:* the mystical syllable AUM (or OM).

16. *Ekam eva advitiyam:* the celebrated formula of the *Chandogya-Upanishad:* "One in truth without second" (non-dual).

17. *Aham, asmi,* "I am".

18. So positive an approach to India's religious and spiritual tradition no doubt will strike some minds as too bold or, at least, too optimistic. In the West in fact, on the strength not only of essayists but also renowned writers, Indians included, Indian thought is very often considered as irremediably inserted in monism and pantheism, and to such a degree that its integration into a Christian theological synthesis seems absolutely out of place. We regret to differ with these authors, but the authentic tradition of India is neither monist nor pantheist, at least not in the sense in which these words are understood in the West at the present time. Nevertheless we do not deny the monist and pantheist tendencies underlying some Indian systems, nor the

frankly monist or pantheist deviation of some modern authors. We simply ask that one should judge Indian thought and spiritual experience in themselves and according to the authentic sources and the Teachers and Sages universally recognized as having outstanding merit. Moreover in the end one perforce must always have recourse to India's scriptures and to the experience of India's great mystics. What in effect the Christian should try to take over from Hinduism is not this or that rite, this or that myth, or this or that theological formulation, but before all else the spiritual experience that is the foundation and the reason for being of all these developments. Moreover one must distrust conceptual and verbal transportations that are made from one culture into another. Even the clearest terms and translations that are the most exact etymologically constantly risk exaggeration if one forgets the halo and the harmonics of the sense and of the experience that accompany these notions and that differ according to the places in which they developed. On the other hand, rarely do those responsible for these translations and transpositions have an equal competence in each of these domains. Thus one more often ends up with approximations whose value the attentive reader must guard himself from over-estimating. Finally—and this remark is the most important of all—one must never forget the essentially provisional value of any philosophy or theology in India. Here philosophy is not a speculative science, conformed to the contemplation of intelligible forms. It is fundamentally "practical" and tends to experience which alone has a beatifying and salvific value. The words and concepts used, for example, by the guru when he teaches his disciple do not aim to transmit doctrinal formulations, but primarily to make him want to desire experience and to provoke in him psychological and mental dispositions most favorable to the spontaneous blossoming of this experience. Words and concepts will never make up for experience, they will always involve antinomies which only direct experience will resolve. Putting too marked an accent on such a point of the formulation to the detriment of others and to speculate on any notion, even one received from Sages, without taking account of the essentially relative character of this notion risks leading to grave errors of interpretation. This is not the place to develop these notations. We recommend the reader to consult two works of mine published by *Éditions du Seuil* and *Éditions du Centurion,* respectively. The first, *Le rencontre de l'hindouisme et du Christianisme* (The Encounter between Hunduism and Christianity) aims to lay the biblical foundations of our "positive" and "assumptive" approach to the spirituality of India. The second, *Sagesse Hindoue, mystique chrétienne* (Hindu Wisdom, Christian mysticism) is an attempt at assumption of the purest *advaitin* experience such as it was lived by one of India's greatest teachers, Sri Ramana Maharishi, in the authentic Christian and trinitary experience.

19. See *Sagesse hindoue, mystique chrétienne* (Paris, Éd. du Centurion).

CHAPTER 5

1. Published in *Carmel,* 1966/IV.
2. All this suggests that there should be a Novitiate at the very start of priestly studies.
3. See for example G. Mury, *Vie spirituelle,* April 1966.

CHAPTER 6

1. Published in *Annales de Sainte Thérèse de Lisieux* Jan. 1970.

CHAPTER 7

1. Published in *Annales de sainte Thérè de Lisieux,* no. 1, January 1972.

PART TWO

1. Mother of Mother-Superior Françcoise-Thérèse of the Carmelite Order of Lisieux, deceased in 1959.

1. Former prioress of the Carmelite Order of Lisieux (1951-1957) and former president of the *Fèdération Sainte-Thérèse de l'Enfant-Jésus"* consolidating the Carmelite Orders of half of northern France, 1953-1968.

1. *Textes mystiques d'Orient et d'Occident* (Mystic texts of the East and West), presented by Solange Lemaitre, Plon, 1935, 3 vols.

1. Mme. L. Charnelet

1. He had just published the *Autobiographical biographies of St. Thérèse of the Child Jesus* (in French) and died accidentally on August 30, 1961.

1. Professed monk of the abbey of Kergonan, residing in the abbey *Sainte-Marie de Paris* from 1951 to 1971.

1. This letter, like the one of December 24, 1955, see above, attests to a certain tension in the relations between Father Monchanin and Father Le Saux. Both were, as Father Le Saux recognized, "personalities too richly endowed and too independent." At that time the question of Shantivanam's future posed itself with a crucial sharpness. The hope of a solution, thanks to the arrival of another "partner" had vanished, and Father Monchanin's state of health already gave disturbing signs. One year after the letter, on October 10, 1957, he died in Paris, and Father Le Saux was soon assigned to the direction of operations in northern India. The future of Shantivanam, however, was assured.

1. Initiation.

1. Benedictine, professed monk of the abbey *Sainte-Marie de Paris,* elected aboot of Ligugé, in 1966.